October 2, 1942.

"...we worked until 3:30 a.m....this was the day! Stanley climbed into the cockpit...a brief wave...and he was off, taxiing to the far end of the field. He turned at the end of his taxi run and ran both engines alternately to maximum speed...a momentary pause while the pilot released the brakes...the jets began to take hold...the plane rolled ever so slowly at first...with us mentally pushing it on...soon began to pick up speed...just opposite us it lifted gently into the air...continued straight away, gaining altitude...past the end of the field...banked and crossed directly over our heads...what a strange feeling...dead silence as it passed directly overhead...then a low rumbling roar like a blow torch...and it was gone, leaving a smell of kerosene in the air...after about ten minutes of low level flight, Bob landed..."

America had entered the Jet Age.

AERO PUBLISHERS, INC.
329 West Aviation Road, Fallbrook, CA 92028

seven decades of progress

A HERITAGE OF AIRCRAFT TURBINE TECHNOLOGY

GENERAL ⊛ ELECTRIC

Manufactured in the United States of America

Book design and production by Advance Studios, Inc.
                    Cincinnati, Ohio

Printed by Printing Service Company
            Dayton, Ohio

Current Printing (last digit)
5   4   3   2

Library of Congress Catalog Card Number: 79-6349

ISBN 0-8168-8355-6

Published by Aero Publishers, Inc.
            Fallbrook, California

CONTENTS

To the memory of Charles Curtis, Sanford Moss, Glenn Warren, Reginald Standerwick, Sam Puffer, Chester Smith, Alan Howard, Truly Warner, Roy Shoults and the other jet pioneers who started it all...

To Jack Parker, Gerhard Neumann, Fred MacFee, Ed Woll for their vision and inspiring leadership in bringing the business to maturity...

To a galaxy of General Electric stars—too numerous to list by name—who identified the goals, created the product, led the charges and solved the problems...

To the thousands of men and women of General Electric and in the industry whose cooperation, creativity and hard work made possible the evolution of turbine technology...

To the future contributors who will write the continuing saga of aircraft turbine engine progress...

this book is respectfully dedicated.

Foreword

Only three generations have passed since that December day in 1903 on the windswept dunes of Kitty Hawk, North Carolina, when the world's first powered aeroplane lifted from the earth and remained aloft for twelve seconds.

In those three generations, however, the speed of earthly transportation has increased forty-fold: from 50 miles an hour to more than 2,000.

In the forefront of this transportation explosion has been the evolution of the aircraft gas turbine—the jet engine. Paralleling the rapid progress in air transportation—indeed, in many cases responsible for it—has been the evolution of General Electric in aircraft propulsion.

For a number of years "progress" has been a term associated with General Electric. And "progress" best describes the seven decades of GE's work in turbine technology.

"Technology is the central strength of the company and continues to be the keystone," according to Reginald H. Jones, General Electric's current chairman of the board and chief executive officer. Today aircraft engines and related services and support account for approximately one tenth of General Electric's total sales.

The documentation of General Electric's contribution to aviation advancement is what this book is about.

In a November 3, 1975 memo, Gerhard Neumann, vice president and group executive of General Electric's Aircraft Engine Group, directed: "I want work to start at once on the history of the Aircraft Engine Group, from Day 1 until now. I would like you to consider a year-by-year event series of whatever was of prime importance."

Since that day four years ago, many people have worked and contributed toward that objective and the result is reflected in these pages. This book is a salute to all those contributors who "made it happen" as well as to the foresight and leadership of Gerhard Neumann.

William R. (Bill) Travers, who was intimately involved in the engineering and marketing of GE aircraft engines for nearly 40 years, undertook the major challenge of research, organization and interviewing. During 1976, Travers talked with more than 100 past and present contributors to General Electric's aircraft engine growth and progress.

The results of Travers' 1976 research led to the establishment of an archive in conjunction with the General Electric Jet Engine Museum at the Evendale, Ohio, plant.

During the next two years, work was directed toward organizing, refining and supplementing the original data. It was clear that the ultimate result of these efforts should be a published documentation —a history book—of General Electric's heritage in turbine technology.

Fred O. MacFee, Jr., in April 1978 was named vice president and group executive of the Aircraft Engine Group. He asked that the history be written and published to serve as printed documentation of the past and perhaps provide a guide for the future.

This volume, like the seven decades of progress in General Electric aircraft turbine technology recorded within its pages, was created by a team of dedicated individuals. The leader of the team that ultimately produced *Seven Decades of Progress* was William A. Schoneberger, who has long been associated with aviation communications. Utilizing the extensive research available as a result of the efforts of Bill Travers and others, as well as his own knowledge of the industry, he provided the principal organization, writing and creative efforts.

The evolution of turbine technology and progress in aviation occurred because of the dedication of thousands of men and women, the great majority of whom go unnamed in this text. The celebration of selected, significant milestones and a few of the names making possible these achievements also serves to celebrate the thousands who are not identified. Only space limitations have precluded the inclusion of the names of all who shared equally in making seven decades of General Electric aircraft gas turbine progress.

The Editors

Leonard A. Dalquest

R. Eric Falk

Ripon W. Haskell

David I. McGinnis

William A. Schoneberger

William R. Travers

December, 1979

The Prelude (1897-1919)...the roots

THE PRELUDE

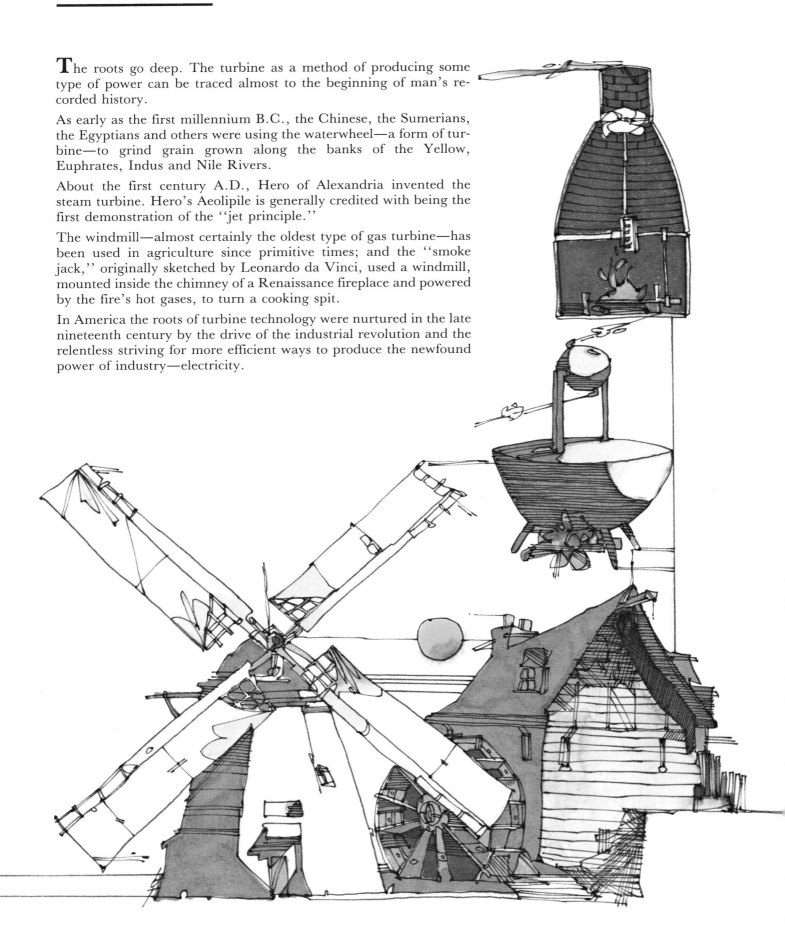

The roots go deep. The turbine as a method of producing some type of power can be traced almost to the beginning of man's recorded history.

As early as the first millennium B.C., the Chinese, the Sumerians, the Egyptians and others were using the waterwheel—a form of turbine—to grind grain grown along the banks of the Yellow, Euphrates, Indus and Nile Rivers.

About the first century A.D., Hero of Alexandria invented the steam turbine. Hero's Aeolipile is generally credited with being the first demonstration of the "jet principle."

The windmill—almost certainly the oldest type of gas turbine—has been used in agriculture since primitive times; and the "smoke jack," originally sketched by Leonardo da Vinci, used a windmill, mounted inside the chimney of a Renaissance fireplace and powered by the fire's hot gases, to turn a cooking spit.

In America the roots of turbine technology were nurtured in the late nineteenth century by the drive of the industrial revolution and the relentless striving for more efficient ways to produce the newfound power of industry—electricity.

1. *Elihu Thomson.*
2. *Charles G. Curtis.*
3. *Thomas A. Edison.*

The first glimmerings of electricity's industrial potential came at the Philadelphia exposition held in the United States' centennial year, 1876. By 1892 a "giant" in the embryonic power generation industry had been formed with the consolidation of two of the major forces in the electrification of America, the Edison General Electric Company and the Thomson-Houston Company. The new General Electric Company was the product of the genius of such men as Thomas A. Edison, Elihu Thomson, Charles A. Coffin, Charles Van Depoele, Edwin W. Rice and later Charles Proteus Steinmetz, William Stanley, Willis R. Whitney and Irving Langmuir. These men were to provide an atmosphere of challenge, encourage the free thinkers and inventive geniuses, establish laboratories that spawned startling innovations and carry on the intellectual curiosity of Thomas Edison.

GE in 1897 began its efforts to use a turbine for generating electric power. The year before, a steam turbine had been patented by Charles G. Curtis, a lawyer turned engineer. Curtis joined GE in 1897 and the company's development of the turbine began.

In 1903 General Electric established the first in a series of turbine technology milestones with the installation at Chicago Edison's Fiske Street Station of the world's largest steam turbine generator. The GE 5,000 kilowatt Curtis-type turbine replaced a reciprocating engine—and large as it was, it occupied only one-tenth the space and was one-eighth the weight and cost one-third as much as its predecessor.

Practical turbine technology had been achieved.

1.

2.

3.

THE PRELUDE

A vision of energy

In 1888, a 16-year-old mechanic, who was later to become one of the "giants" on whose shoulders General Electric would build in the 1920s, '30s and '40s, had an idea that if fuel could be burned in compressed air, the energy output would be increased tremendously.

Sanford A. Moss, born in San Francisco in 1872, took his idea to the University of California and by 1900 had earned his bachelor's and master's degrees. Traveling cross-country at the turn of the century, Moss began work on his PhD at Cornell University. For his doctoral thesis, young Moss began theoretical examination of the gas turbine and, in laboratory experiments conducted in 1903, achieved what no other man had successfully done previously: produce energy to operate a turbine by burning gas in a pressurized chamber.

Moss' experiments at Cornell were conducted in a laboratory directly under the office of one of the more prominent members of the University faculty, Dr. William F. Durand.

The young doctoral candidate's experiments created fumes, explosions and some disgusting odors—to the great annoyance of Professor Durand. With some considerable feeling, the Professor announced to anyone within earshot that "whatever Moss was doing, it was not likely to be worth the noise, smoke and smells." In fact, Professor Durand predicted, it was likely to be "worth nothing at all."

But, Dr. Moss' doctoral thesis on the gas turbine succeeded in attracting the attention of GE engineers who were already involved in the new technology of steam turbines for power generation. It was a natural association. The young Cornell graduate began his more than 40-year career with the General Electric Company.

Only 14 years later, in the tense atmosphere of the U.S. entry into the first World War—and again in 1941, immediately prior to the U.S. involvement in the second World War—Dr. Durand would have occasion to remember the student who had seemed so hopeless.

1.

1. *Sanford A. Moss, age 22, 1894.*

2. *College of Mechanics, class of 1896. University of California, Berkeley. Moss standing, rear left.*

200 years of turbine evolution

Although the roots of turbine technology date to the wind and water driven machinery of the Chinese, to the Middle East, to Hero and da Vinci, the first practical applications of steam and gas turbines did not emerge until the 18th and 19th centuries. A patent for a gas turbine operating on a cycle similar to present-day units was issued to John Barber in England in 1791.

The first commercially significant steam turbine was built by William Avery in the United States in 1831.

The action/reaction principle of today's aircraft gas turbine engine had already been spelled out by Sir Isaac Newton in his "Principia," published in 1687. Newton's Third Law of Motion—"For every action, there is a reaction, equal in force and opposite in direction"—explains in very simple terms why jet airplanes move through the air.

In the 1880s, Sir Charles Parsons of England and Carl G. P. de Laval of Sweden each demonstrated significant progress in steam turbine technology with practical turbines. And, in the 1890s, A.C.E. Rateau of France, who was to be involved in the development of "boosters" for internal combustion aircraft engines in World War I, developed a simplified working steam turbine.

The first demonstration of the present type of gas turbine was made in 1872 by F. Stolze of Germany. Another German, Hans Holzwarth, began work in 1905 on an explosion-type turbine utilizing a principle not unlike that of today's gas turbine combustion chambers. And, in 1908, René Lorin of France proposed an extremely heavy combustion jet engine somewhat similar in concept to today's jet engines.

2.

THE PRELUDE

Moss pioneers at General Electric

At the same time British, French and German inventors were struggling with the development and production of practical and efficient gas turbines, Dr. Moss in the United States was striving to use the principles of his Cornell thesis to interest his employers at GE in further gas turbine research. His efforts were thwarted by the limitations of the materials and designs of that time. The lack of high temperature metals and low efficiencies of both air compressors and turbines were an imposing deterrent. The energy output of a compressor linked with a turbine—although intriguing—was simply not sufficient for the fuel expended. The research was temporarily shelved.

Dr. Moss had been assigned to the company's Lynn, Massachusetts, Steam Turbine department. The Lynn Works had been the headquarters of the Thomson-Houston Company as GE's Schenectady Works had been headquarters of the Edison General Electric Company until the 1892 consolidation that created GE.

At Lynn, Dr. Moss was fortunate to receive his initial exposure to one of the great pioneers of the electrical and turbine industries, Elihu Thomson, who was then devoting much of his time to research at the Lynn Engineering Laboratory. In addition to Thomson, Dr. Moss also had the opportunity to work with Charles P. Steinmetz, an imposing figure in the long line of GE "wizards." In this atmosphere a team of dedicated turbine technologists, initially under the leadership of Dr. Moss, would carry forward in the next seven decades the advancements leading to turbine powered flight.

The young engineer was asked to turn his talents to the design of air compressors and, by 1917, GE had built a successful and thriving business producing centrifugal compressors for blast furnaces, pneumatic conveyors, yeast manufacture and other applications which required low-pressure compressed air in large quantities.

With success achieved in these first ventures into commercial products, Dr. Moss returned to his first love—research. He established the Turbine Research department (later the famous Thomson Laboratory) within the Lynn Steam Turbine department. His early-1900s studies of gas turbines and compressors were dusted off and work began in earnest on theoretical and mechanical development.

2.

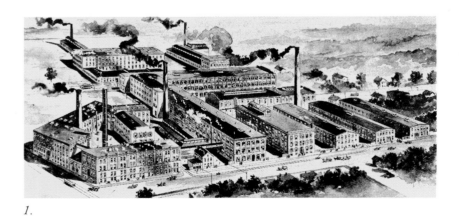

3.

1.

When the U.S. entered the first World War in April, 1917, GE management quickly put Dr. Moss' Turbine Research department to work on submarine detectors, centrifugal machine guns and methods of detonating enemy torpedoes before they struck.

In the fall of 1917, the echoes of Dr. Moss' 1903 experiments reverberated in Washington, D.C. His one-time Cornell professor, William F. Durand, now head of the newly-formed National Advisory Committee for Aeronautics, summoned the GE engineer to the nation's capital and started General Electric and Moss on their first venture into aviation.

1. *Lynn River Works, circa 1892.*
2. *Dr. Moss.*
3. *Charles Proteus Steinmetz.*
4. *LePere P-59 biplane with GE turbosupercharger (above propeller).*

4.

THE PRELUDE

GE turbine technology goes to war

In 1906 a Swiss engineer, Alfred Buechi, had first proposed the idea of an engine ''booster'' to his employers, Brown-Boveri. His basic concept was that the exhaust gases of a piston engine could be used to drive a turbine wheel linked to a compressor which, in turn, would supply compressed air back to the engine, boosting its power at higher altitudes where air is thinner and has less pressure. Buechi's idea was tested in 1911, but the Swiss lost interest. By 1916 the idea had been taken over by a Frenchman, Auguste C.E. Rateau, and the concept of the first aircraft engine turbo-supercharger—or booster—was put to practical application. French aircraft equipped with these engine boosters were used over no-man's-land before the Great War ended.

When the U.S. entered the war, the details of the Rateau design were turned over to the National Advisory Committee for Aeronautics. Fortunately, Dr. Durand recalled his young student's work of 14 years before and, being well aware of General Electric's pioneering work with compressors and turbines, proposed that the company would be the logical choice to develop and test an aircraft engine booster based on the Rateau concept.

Representing the company, Dr. Moss quickly accepted the Durand challenge.

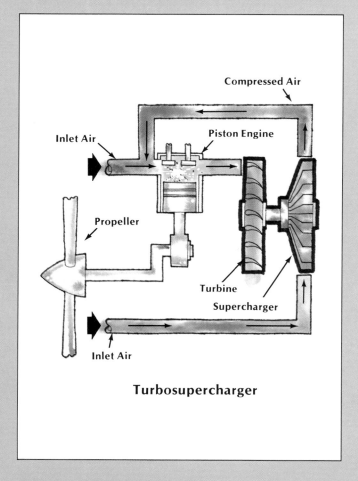

Turbosupercharger

One of GE's first defense program competitions soon evolved. The U.S. company representing Professor Rateau insisted that they, too, be allowed to develop the engine booster for the Army. Both companies were awarded contracts and the development work proceeded rapidly under the pressure and secrecy of wartime. American pilots were already in France flying Spads and Nieuports and the fledgling U.S. aviation "industry" was gearing up to produce combat aircraft.

Work on both designs continued through the end of 1917 and into 1918. As the superchargers began to take shape, the Rateau and Moss designs differed in one key concept. The Rateau design called for the turbine—which naturally operated at very high temperatures—to be enclosed in a metal casing without provisions for cooling. This was a common practice with steam turbines operating at considerably lower temperatures. Dr. Moss, drawing on his Cornell experiments and the practical research in the Lynn Engineering Laboratory, contended that the turbine wheel should operate with a casing designed so that cooling air could be provided. That design difference was to prove ultimately consequential.

French turbosupercharged TP-1, circa World War I.

THE PRELUDE

The Army, recognizing the competitive nature of the development and feeling the pressures of the ongoing war, called for a test demonstration. A winner would be selected on the basis of the test results. The test specified called for an engine to run at full speed at sea level for 15 minutes. The Rateau forces agreed to the specifications. Moss disagreed.

The true test of the turbosupercharger was its ability to run at altitude, contended Dr. Moss. That meant a sea level test would be invalid. He proposed the test be conducted on the highest accessible mountaintop in the United States. As a result, Pikes Peak (altitude: 14,109 feet) became famous as a technology landmark as well as for its scenic beauty and geographic distinction.

The logistics required for testing at such a remote site were awesome: an engine test mount, fuel tanks, instruments, a machine shop, spare parts and provisions for the test crew had to be assembled and transported nearly two and a half miles vertically. Congress appropriated funds. A Liberty engine was carefully pre-calibrated at McCook Field, Dayton, Ohio, to produce its rated 350 horsepower at sea level. When the entire rig was finally transported to the top of Pikes Peak, the engine was test run without a supercharger. It produced only 230 horsepower. Clearly the supercharger's challenge was established.

Experiments with the competing designs began June 19, 1918, and continued through the summer and fall. With weather conditions worsening atop the mountain peak, the tests finally were concluded on October 17. The GE-supercharged engine ultimately produced 356 horsepower—six more than at sea level—and, most important, was in good condition at the conclusion of the test. The Moss design had been proven. The Army announced it would proceed with the GE design. The company had won its first of many military aviation competitions.

The jubilation of technological success was short-lived, however. In the wake of the signing of the Armistice on November 11, 1918, the government cancelled all military development contracts.

1. Moss, center, with U.S. Army and GE team atop Pikes Peak, 1918.
2. Preparing to start the turbosupercharged Liberty engine.

2.

1.

In a little more than a year and a half, General Electric had both won and lost its first government contracts for aircraft turbine power. But the stage had been set. A hard core of visionaries, including a cadre of GE scientists, was not going to let this startling innovation—a portent of the future—stop there.

In the postwar regrouping of 1919, a decision was made in the Army Air Corps' Power Plant Laboratory at McCook Field (now Wright-Patterson Air Force Base, Dayton) that would assure the continued evolution of aircraft propulsion for the next 20 years.

Largely through the efforts of Lieutenant E. T. Jones, then head of the Power Plant Laboratory, Opie Chenoweth, assistant engineer, and A. L. Berger, supercharger installation mechanic, the Army selected the GE turbosupercharger as one of its key development projects for the future.

In 1919 a contract was signed that called for a GE-supercharged Liberty engine to maintain its sea level rating (by then it was 400 horsepower) at altitudes up to 20,000 feet.

General Electric and the Lynn team headed by Dr. Moss moved with confidence into the 1920s.

The Twenties...years of struggle

THE TWENTIES

Dayton, Ohio—home of the bicycle shop where the Wright brothers conceived their aeroplane (It wasn't until 1963 that the Encyclopaedia Britannica officially recognized the spelling ''airplane'' in their editions) and today billed as the ''cradle of aviation'' —was the site of at least three significant milestones in the early evolution of U.S. aircraft turbine technology.

The first was the Army's 1919 decision to continue development of the turbosupercharger despite the end of the Great War and the apparently lessened need for military aircraft—as a result of the vision and persistence of Army Air Corps Power Plant Laboratory personnel at McCook Field in Dayton.

In less than two years, this decision led directly to two new world altitude records set in the skies above Dayton in 1920 and 1921— and the resultant confidence that superchargers would push the frontiers of flight higher, faster and farther.

1.

2.

16

1. *Dr. Moss; Lieutenant G.W. Elsey, observer; Major R.W. Schroeder, chief test pilot; prior to 1920 record flight.*

2. *Lieutenant J.A. Macready, pilot; Dr. Moss; Captain G.E.A. Hallett; A.L. "Doc" Berger, AAC Power Plant Lab; with GE supercharged LePere biplane prior to nearly eight-mile-high 1921 flight.*

Into the wild blue yonder

The visionaries of the Power Plant Laboratory—particularly A.L. "Doc" Berger, who was to play a significant role in the U.S. military as a "champion" of the turbosupercharger from the days of World War I right through World War II—had convinced their chain of command to pursue the expanding vistas created by the linking of the turbine with the piston engine.

By early 1920, the GE/Army Air Corps team was ready to test fly the improved GE supercharger that had been contracted for in 1919. Installed in a LePere biplane—one of the most advanced of the day—the 400 horsepower liquid-cooled Liberty engine with the GE turbosupercharger made an historic flight February 27, 1920.

The pilot, Major Rudolph Schroeder, climbed rapidly and at 25,000 feet could see from his open cockpit the ice forming on the wings. Schroeder kept the biplane in a nose up attitude and tried to maintain control in the thin, 60-below-zero air. At the peak of his climb—33,133 feet—the major lost consciousness. The airplane nosed over, slid off on one wing and began an uncontrolled descent. At about 4,000 feet, in a scene later to be restaged in hundreds of Hollywood aviation thrillers, the richer, oxygen-filled air revived the pilot and he managed to bring the test aircraft to a safe landing.

By setting a new world altitude mark, Major Schroeder, the Army Air Corps and General Electric had proved that the turbosupercharger could "kid" an airplane engine into believing it was still flying at sea level where the higher air pressure was more conducive to its efficient—and power-producing—performance.

Just as with many pioneering test pilots of future generations, Major Schroeder nearly perished in the historic flight. The effects of insufficient oxygen and sub-zero temperatures in the open cockpit flight sent the pilot to the hospital for an extended recovery.

Encouraged by the success of the 1920 flight, GE and the Army made further improvements in the turbo, the engine and the airplane. The next year, the Army Air Corps' Lieutenant J.A. Macready set another new world altitude mark, piloting his LePere aircraft into the skies nearly a mile and a half beyond the Schroeder mark, to 40,800 feet.

The small band of aircraft gas turbine pioneers believed that, like the airplanes they had pushed beyond previous limitations, they could now "take off" with their development.

THE TWENTIES

The struggle ahead

Although the Army had placed an order for 150 turbos with GE, company interest in the program in the early 1920s was overshadowed by the rapid advancements being made in electric power generation, industrial equipment, home appliances and lighting. A period of postwar economic expansion and a return-to-peacetime-pursuits psychology were upon the land.

Within GE, the aircraft gas turbine pioneers who had performed all of their early work under the aegis of the Steam Turbine department at Lynn now found themselves producing the Army's turbos in the Street Lighting department. Steam Turbine was too busy with commercial work to provide manufacturing space. Reginald G. Standerwick, who was to play a significant role in the first U.S.-developed jet engine in 1941-42, did the engineering on these early turbosuperchargers.

On the research side, Dr. Moss and a team of men who were to shape the evolution of the aircraft gas turbine at GE for the next 25-30 years comprised the Mechanical Research department of Lynn's Thomson Laboratory. Waverly A. Reeves, M.G. ''Robbie'' Robinson, Chester W. Smith and Sam Puffer were all to contribute heavily to GE's gas turbine work in the next quarter-century.

As with much of the company's early research and development work, the Lynn and Schenectady Works—reflecting the legacy of General Electric's beginnings—each contributed to the progress. Working at Schenectady was a young University of Wisconsin graduate who had joined the company in 1919 on GE's Test Engineering Program. He proposed in the early 1920s that gas turbine research for industrial use be started there. Glenn B. Warren, while a Wisconsin student in 1914, had written a memo to himself that he would one day build a successful gas turbine. He had already built two turbine combustion chambers in his garage.

Another of the ''giants'' of GE's '20s, '30s and '40s, Glenn Warren would become vice president and general manager of the company's Turbine division as well as the driving force behind a major business decision the company made in the 1940s that would help assure the progress leading to GE's present position in world aviation.

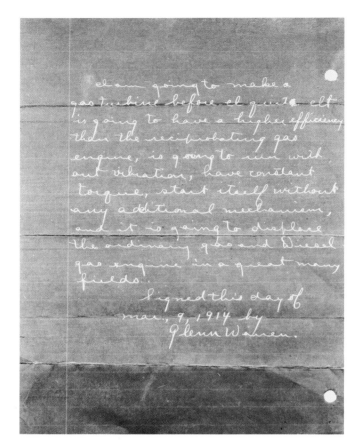

1.

Billy Mitchell proves a point

Progress on turbosuperchargers in the United States was proceeding at a snail's pace. But one historic event in the early '20s added a significant measure of credibility to the worth of turbos. Moreover, it demonstrated a military strategy that would prove a decisive factor in the Allied victory following the harrowing days of World War II.

In the now-famous debate over the value of airpower in wartime, then-Colonel Billy Mitchell was faced with a challenge. He contended that bomb-carrying aircraft were more effective than surface guns against naval targets. In order to prove his point, the War Department told him his airplanes would have to fly no lower than 15,000 feet to avoid assumed antiaircraft fire and his targets would be anchored at sea in an unspecified location 100 miles from land. Confronted with what appeared to be insurmountable odds, Colonel Mitchell ordered turbosuperchargers installed on the Martin bombers he planned to use for the test. The boosters, Mitchell believed, would provide the range and altitude he would need.

The German battleships Ostfriesland and Frankfurt, which had been captured in World War I, were towed 100 miles off the Virginia Capes to serve as targets. On July 21, 1921, Mitchell's flight of GE-turbosupercharged bombers took off to seek and destroy the dreadnaughts.

Mitchell's airplanes found their targets and dropped their bombs from above the 15,000-foot minimum. The Ostfriesland sank three minutes after a final hit; the Frankfurt went to the bottom 30 minutes later.

Billy Mitchell—with an assist from GE turbos—had made his point that day in 1921. But it was to be another 20-plus years before his revolutionary beliefs were positively demonstrated and his strategic military contribution recognized.

1. *Glenn Warren's 1914 student memo.*
2. *Martin MB-1 bomber used for historic 1921 demonstration.*
3. *William E. Mitchell.*

3.

2.

THE TWENTIES

The struggle continues...very slowly

Despite the dramatic demonstration of gas turbine advantages in the Dayton skies and off the Virginia Capes in 1921-22, there were few significant advances during the balance of the decade.

One major reason, of course, was the emphasis on peacetime production and commercial products. General Electric was concentrating its turbine business efforts on steam turbines for both electric power generation and naval propulsion. The world's first turbine electric ship, equipped by GE, reduced by two days the New York-Gibraltar sailing time on its initial voyage in 1921. And the USS Maryland, equipped with two GE turbine generators of 11,000 kilowatts each, was one of the most powerful ships in the world. The Maryland's generators were capable of providing enough energy to supply a city of 100,000 people.

In 1925 one of the first non-aviation spinoffs of the turbosupercharger made the nation's headlines. Peter DePaolo, driving a Duesenberg Special with a GE supercharger designed by Dr. Moss and his team of researchers at Lynn's Thomson Laboratory, won the Indianapolis 500 that year.

The other major reason for the lack of progress in aircraft turbos in the U.S. during the 1920s was a changing philosophy within the aviation industry.

Charles A. Lindbergh's New York-Paris solo flight in 1927 had underscored the industry's belief that air cooling of engines would replace liquid cooling. Most aircraft engines such as the Liberty engine were liquid cooled. With the advent of air cooled engines, the leading U.S. powerplant manufacturers, Pratt & Whitney and Wright Aeronautical, elected not to add the extra weight and complexity of the hot exhaust pipes required for turbine-driven superchargers. Still convinced, however, that superchargers were necessary, their designers built gear-driven compressors within the framework of the new, air cooled engines.

General Electric worked closely with the engine companies and eventually developed a small but significant business from the research, development and production of impellers and diffuser plates used in these engines. The company would continue this segment of aircraft supercharger production until the mid-1940s.

Dr. Moss, Professor Elihu Thomson, Colonel Charles A. Lindbergh at Lynn River Works, 1930.

Gas turbines as the primary source of airplane power?

The gas turbine had been linked to airplanes for the first time during World War I. That linking of turbine "boost" with piston engines had set the stage for the evolution during the next 60 years of a source of propulsion that would enable airplanes to achieve speeds, altitudes and distances never before envisioned.

The dream of using gas turbines as the principal source of aircraft engine power may have been in the minds of some of the early visionaries, but apparently the first time this dream was "officially" recognized was in Great Britain in the 1920s.

Early in that decade an engineer working for Britain's Royal Aircraft Establishment (RAE) evolved a new theory based on the science of airfoils. (An airplane's wing is an "airfoil" and exemplifies its thicker-and-rounded-at-the-leading-edge and curved-and-thinner-as-it-tapers-to-the-trailing-edge principle.) Using a "straight through" axial flow compressor and turbine combination with a combustion chamber, A.A. Griffith believed he could design a system efficient enough to turn an airplane propeller.

In 1926, the RAE provided Griffith funds to carry out "preliminary experiments to verify the theory." By 1929 he had built by hand components that demonstrated remarkable efficiencies during early testing in the RAE's wind tunnels. He requested additional money to continue development. Although not fully funded, in 1930 an OK was given to continue research on turbocompressor and combustion principles. But by 1931, the worldwide Depression had hit and what little RAE funding remained was directed toward continuing advancement of piston engines.

The action/reaction propulsion concept in Britain was not limited to the Royal Aircraft Establishment. In 1928, a young Royal Air Force officer in his fourth term at the RAF college at Cranwell wrote a thesis putting forth the theory that rocket propulsion might be feasible for high altitude, high speed flight.

A year later, this same RAF officer conceived a combination of the gas turbine and jet propulsion. In 1930 Frank Whittle was granted a British patent for the concept—but no funds. The name Frank Whittle and "jet propulsion" had first become inextricably linked as the decade of the 1920s ended.

Technology stirs

The decade of the '20s had been a period of slow, often frustrating, progress for aircraft gas turbine evolution. The technology was stirring but the market was far from ready.

The Thirties...decade of budding ideas

THE THIRTIES

The Great Depression settled over the land in the early 1930s. Both industry and government suffered from its debilitating effects. Yet in spite of the severe cutbacks in all types of spending, the leaders of the U.S. Army Air Corps' Power Plant Laboratory believed they must look to the future of military aviation and continue development of the turbine technology advances made in the 1920s.

In September, 1931, the Army awarded General Electric a contract for testing high temperature turbine nozzle and blade combinations. The company built its first high temperature test stand under this contract. Work continued on this significant facet of gas turbine evolution throughout the '30s as a result of contract renewals in 1935 and 1939. Although the research performed was primarily in support of turbosuperchargers, the connection to gas turbines as a primary power source was abundantly clear.

"Red-hot buckets [turbine blades] in operation were continuously exhibited to Wright Field and General Electric officials explicitly as gas turbine propaganda [for aircraft propulsion]," Dr. Moss later said.

1. Curtiss XP-23 biplane with external turbosupercharger on engine cowling, 1932.

2. TWA Northrop Gamma, chief pilot "Tommy" Tomlinson, 1937.

1.

Turbines create a civil/military marriage

Turbosuperchargers made mighty strides in this ten-year period—helping make possible in the 1940s "over the weather" passenger flight as well as high altitude, multi-engine strategic military aircraft. And in the last year of the decade of the '30s, gas turbine evolution was to achieve an historic milestone: the world's first jet powered flight.

At GE work continued on components for the geared (or internal) supercharger of the type used on the Pratt & Whitney and Wright engines of the period.

These superchargers worked reasonably well at the relatively low altitudes then being flown but, as airplane and engine designers reached for higher and higher altitudes, the geared supercharger became increasingly complex. It added unwanted weight and penalized takeoff power by using more fuel than the turbine-driven supercharger. Dr. Moss' turbo found the tide of technology evolution turning in its direction.

Just as they had so often in the past—and would so frequently in the future—economic and political requirements provided the impetus for the acceleration of technology advancement. Following the lull in the '20s, renewed interest in turbosuperchargers was generated in the '30s as both civil and military aviation began to see the value of higher altitude—and more efficient—flight.

The military planners envisioned the need for high altitude flight, but had no specific aircraft developments on which it could be demonstrated. The growing commercial air transport field presented just such an opportunity.

By 1936 U.S. airlines had already carried more than a million passengers. Expansion of this exciting mode of travel was hampered severely, however, by the hesitation of many potential air travelers. The frequent turbulence and resultant air sickness encountered at low altitude flight was a hindrance to the less hardy. In addition, air carriers frequently found themselves forced to cancel scheduled revenue flights because of bad weather.

Airplane designers and airline executives agreed that if they could fly over the weather, air travel would be both more comfortable and more reliable. The turbosupercharger could make that possible.

These needs came together in the mid-'30s in what may have been the first example of civil-military-industry cooperation. An Army/TWA/Northrop/GE alliance was created to test a turbosupercharger at high altitude. The airplane selected was a TWA Northrop Gamma designed by John K. Northrop in the tradition of his pacesetting Alpha concept of the 1920s. The Alpha was the world's first all-metal, monocoque fuselage aircraft (in which the fuselage becomes the load-bearing member, eliminating the internal struts and wires of the early airplanes). The Gamma—a heavier, larger and greater capacity monocoque airplane with a more powerful engine than the Alpha—was just right for demonstrating the turbo's capabilities.

2.

At the insistence of engine and aviation industry experts, GE had taken out as much weight as possible from the supercharger. The first two tests failed because the "lightened" turbine wheel disintegrated. Discouragement and frustration almost caused cancellation of the entire venture. But GE engineers Moss, Puffer and Smith maintained they could make it work. A new turbine wheel was quickly built in Lynn.

The new design was personally delivered to the site of the tests in Kansas City and installed on the Gamma by Waverly Reeves, who had been in charge of the 1918 Pikes Peak test. Reeves had never flown, despite his close association with the young industry.

After the new turbine wheel was installed, TWA pilot D.W. "Tommy" Tomlinson, chief pilot of the airline and widely known for his skill and courage, asked Reeves if this one would work. Reeves assured him it would. Tomlinson challenged Reeves' confidence in what everyone connected with the test believed would be a last ditch effort by telling him, "If you believe it will work this time, the best way to find out is to go along with me on the flight!"

Showing not the slightest hesitation, Reeves climbed into the baggage compartment with the observer and was quickly briefed on the use of oxygen at altitude. Tomlinson taxied out. On July 5, 1937, the Gamma took off from Kansas City, heading for Dayton, Ohio. Some minutes later the airplane had reached 37,000 feet with the new turbine wheel—and its two "passengers," Reeves and the observer—intact.

The flight was not without incident, however. Halfway to Dayton, the observer's oxygen tank failed and the man passed out. Reeves frantically tried to signal Tomlinson in the cockpit. It was an open cockpit and wind noise made communication impossible. Thinking quickly, Reeves shared his own oxygen mask and revived the observer. They continued this alternating "buddy" system all the way into Dayton. Reeves wondered if all flying was like this.

The first "over the weather" flight between distant cities had been accomplished. The turbosupercharger had once again proved its value.

TWA and Captain Tomlinson, using the GE-turbosupercharged Northrop Gamma, continued extensive research into high altitude flying. The results of these ongoing tests established the basic design specifications for the first four-engine transport capable of flying above the weather.

1.

1. The turbosupercharger team, in the 1940s: S.R. Puffer; E.S. Thompson; R.G. Standerwick; Dr. S.A. Moss; W.A. Reeves; C.H. Auger.

2. GE-turbosupercharged Boeing 299 on cross-country flight.

2.

Turbos begin to impact on military aircraft design

The TWA Gamma tests provided the Army Air Corps with the evidence it needed to move ahead with turbosupercharger development and production. Army planners had already laid down specifications for the first four-engine, long range bomber in history—the Boeing Model 299, forerunner of the famed B-17 "Flying Fortress."

GE received a contract for production of 230 units of the improved "Type B" turbosupercharger—a new design that would enable a 1,000 horsepower engine to maintain full power up to 25,000 feet.

It was decision time for General Electric management. Until then, all of the turbo development work had been centered in Lynn's Thomson Laboratory. But this order was well beyond the scope of a "lab" operation. In late 1937, the Supercharger department was officially created. The company had put the stamp of recognition on its aviation pioneers.

Sam Puffer, one of Dr. Moss' original 1921 team, was named designing engineer. Dr. Chester Smith, another of the Moss cadre from the Thomson Mechanical Research group, joined the department as leading scientist and Gus Berg was placed in charge of manufacturing. Puffer, Smith and Berg were to continue as leading players in the years ahead—through the difficult days of World War II.

The application of the GE turbos to the B-17 proved a real challenge—and some substantial hurdles had to be overcome. The turbos were first installed on top of the wings. That proved undesirable because it hindered aircraft performance. They were moved to the bottom of the wings and the situation improved greatly—until another crisis developed. The turbine blades began to pull out of the wheel as a result of distortion caused by excessive exhaust temperatures from the air cooled engines.

In Lynn, Dr. Smith and associates—in a frenzied redesign effort— looked for ways to cool the turbine. Boeing and the Air Corps were becoming impatient. Flight testing of the B-17 was being curtailed: altitude restrictions of 15,000 feet were placed on the flights. Boeing told the Air Corps the B-17 had been "a good airplane" until the turbos were added and official paperwork was put into channels giving Boeing permission to begin delivering production B-17s without turbos.

Dr. Smith's team successfully created a new cooling technique to protect the critical section of the turbine blades. And, just as in the classic Western movie cavalry charge, Waverly Reeves of Pikes Peak and TWA Gamma fame—now a seasoned air traveler— flew from Lynn to Seattle with the new Smith-designed turbines. He saw them installed, and watched as successful flight testing saved the day. The B-17 maintained its full power well above the required 25,000 feet and its air speed exceeded all expectations. Although the planners and designers could not know it at the time, the B-17 was ready to meet the challenge of its worth in a conflict that was just then beginning to take form on the world political scene.

As a result of the B-17 experience, the Air Corps ordered turbosuperchargers for installation on aircraft that would prove decisive in the ensuing air action: Lockheed's P-38 Lightning, Consolidated's B-24 Liberator, Republic's P-47 Thunderbolt, and, eventually, the Boeing B-29 Superfortress.

During the 1930s, the gas turbine—at least as it helped to boost the performance of piston engines—had finally outgrown the Thomson Laboratory. General Electric began to study ways to expand capabilities.

THE THIRTIES

Gas turbines for primary power...still in the lab

If turbosuperchargers had moved out of the laboratory in the '30s, basic gas turbine research and the hint of gas turbine use as a primary source of power certainly had not.

The Army Air Corps' Power Plant Laboratory and GE's Thomson Laboratory, in conjunction with their joint development of the supercharger, had been sharing design ideas and concepts of gas turbines for aircraft propulsion. Sam Puffer later recalled, "...ever since the start of this work on gas turbine performance, there had occurred numerous... conversations and meetings [with Wright Field] at which the probability of an ultimate gas turbine for aircraft propulsion was discussed...." The company had been asked to make recommendations as to how this development could proceed, Puffer noted, and the hurdle remained the lack of suitable materials as well as low compressor efficiencies.

In 1936 Wright Field prepared a report, "The Gas Turbine as a Prime Mover for Aircraft." In 1936 and 1937, GE completed several research bulletins and engineering reports on gas turbines for stationary powerplants. In February, 1937, GE submitted a paper to Wright Field entitled "Gas Turbine Power Plants for Aeronautical Applications" that focused on using the gas turbine to drive a propeller—certainly one of the first studies of the turboprop engine.

The minutes of a GE Schenectady Engineering Council meeting convened in April, 1939, include this statement by Sam Puffer: "If the General Electric should present a good design for an airplane gas turbine equipment to the government, it would be likely to result in a development order without specific guarantees. And...any development along that line would be applicable to a locomotive at a later date."

In the summer of 1939, a study was prepared in Lynn on "Jet Propulsion Gas Turbines" and forwarded to Schenectady to Dale D. Streid—later to become one of GE's best known jet engine technologists—for comment. Although Streid was "pessimistic" at the outset about this use of gas turbines because of the high temperatures required, he was invited to Lynn and became convinced of the gas turbine's potential for aircraft. In September, 1939, Streid wrote optimistically about jet propulsion for speeds of 450 miles per hour or more in a memo with the prophetic heading, "Airplane Propulsion by Means of a Jet Reaction and Gas Turbine Power Plant."

In the mid-1930s Dr. Moss had been in England and he reported on the gas turbine work under way at British Thomson-Houston (an offspring of the original U.S. company), including some of the early "exhaust gas turbines...for airplane service." Moss had observed the initial Whittle efforts.

The compilation of data...the exchange of ideas... the sharing of technology breakthoughs...had begun. The first glimmerings of jet flight had been taking place on both sides of the Atlantic in the decade of the 1930s.

1.

2.

Parallel—but separate—developments

Gas turbine work progressed slowly in the U.S. in the '30s. But Britain and Germany—independently and unknown to each other—were making rapid progress in turbines as a primary source of aircraft propulsion. Despite their separate developments, Britain and Germany shared a common motivation: military requirements.

In Germany, Hans von Ohain, a University of Göttingen aerodynamics student, patented a turbojet engine design in 1935. While similar to Whittle's concept, it was different in many details. In 1936, von Ohain's professor, who knew Ernst Heinkel, president of the famous Heinkel aircraft company, prevailed upon him to hire the young student to develop the engine. A 550-pound thrust engine was built and demonstrated by March, 1937, convincing the company that work should proceed on a flight engine. Von Ohain began work on a 1,980-pound thrust engine and the aircraft designers laid plans for an airframe to utilize the powerplant.

When the first engine did not meet specifications, a modified version producing 1,100 pounds of thrust was built and substituted in the completed He 178 airframe.

In total secrecy—even from Third Reich officials in Berlin—plans were made for a first flight at dawn on a Sunday morning in August, 1939. The site chosen was a Heinkel airfield at Marienehe near the north coast of Germany, along the Baltic. At that latitude, the sun rose about four a.m. in the summer.

An active Luftwaffe test pilot who was also attached to the Heinkel staff, Erich Warsitz, had been chosen for the flight. Because of Ernst Heinkel's impatience, no preliminary taxi tests were made. When Warsitz was convinced the engine was not going to explode as he made his ground runup, he taxied out for the flight, a cloud of dust from the jet exhaust trailing behind him. Within seconds, the He 178, powered by von Ohain's He S-3b turbojet engine, lifted from the Marienehe runway. The world's first jet flight was underway—August 27, 1939.

Although Warsitz encountered trouble retracting the landing gear, the engine performed without flaw. After a relatively short, low level flight, he landed the He 178, finally bringing it to a stop on the runway—just short of the Warnow River.

Five days later—September 1, 1939—Hitler's armies invaded Poland. The gas turbine development race took on a new urgency.

1. Dale D. Streid.

2. World's first jet aircraft, Heinkel He 178, flew August 27, 1939.

3. Hans von Ohain.

3.

Whittle's determination — and struggle

Meanwhile, in Britain, RAF officer Frank Whittle already had a 1930 British patent for his jet engine.

His decade-long struggle against the bureaucracy and the "snicker/can't-do-that" philosophy had begun in that year. Reporting his patent to the Air Ministry—as required of a military officer—he received discouraging news: the government was not interested. As a result, the invention was not classified under any secrecy order and, in a year and a half, the details soon began appearing in technical journals—including some in Germany and the U.S.

Whittle applied for and was enrolled in advanced engineering studies at Peterhouse College, Cambridge. During this time, his patent came up for renewal. Whittle, with a growing family and the world still in the throes of a depression, couldn't afford the five pounds renewal fee. The patent lapsed.

But help arrived unexpectedly in 1935. An ex-Royal Air Force officer who knew Whittle and remembered his convictions about the jet engine and another former RAF officer offered to support and promote Whittle's efforts. By the fall, the investment house of O.T. Falk & Partners, Ltd. had agreed to finance the project and the firm of Power Jets Ltd. was formed. Power Jets then let a design contract to British Thomson-Houston, where Dr. Moss and others from GE saw the engine work during their visits to BTH.

Work continued at BTH for nearly four years. The RAF had given tacit approval (but no funds or recognition) to the project by permitting the young flight officer to devote part-time effort to the Power Jets firm.

Whittle and his team of pioneers had recurring problems in the combustion and turbine sections, including turbine failures and even engine explosions. BTH employees, in fear because of the sounds, smells and vibrations caused by the engine testing, complained to their management. Whittle and his "folly" were dispatched to an empty BTH factory near Coventry.

Finally, in July, 1939, the Air Ministry awarded Power Jets a contract for an experimental jet engine to power a specially designed airplane which Gloster Aircraft Company would build. The engine, designated W-1, was to develop 855 pounds of thrust. The aircraft was designated the E.28/39. The engine/airframe combination would set the stage for the Allies' first jet flight in the next decade.

1.

2.

The end of an eventful decade

As the '30s came to a close, the gas turbine seeds that had been sown in the late 1800s were finally beginning to bud...some more vigorously than others...but all were coming to life.

In Germany, a jet powered aircraft had already flown. In Britain, hardware for an engine had been built and tested; an airplane was in the design stages. In the U.S., gas turbine work had been concentrated on turbosuperchargers, but a handful of Army Air Corps and GE visionaries had taken the first steps toward the realization of a true jet powerplant.

Japan began gas turbine work in 1937 when the Japanese Navy purchased Swiss Brown-Boveri engines with an eye toward adapting them for aviation use. Italy started gas turbine studies in 1933 when engineer Secondo Campini proposed the use of an airplane fuselage as a giant cylinder for aircraft jet propulsion. The other key protagonists of a soon-to-be declared World War II were reacting to military requirements with increased action.

1. *Sir Frank Whittle, circa 1955.*
2. *Gloster E.28/39, powered by Whittle's W-1, first flew May 15, 1941.*
3. *Messerschmidt Me262, Germany's first operational jet.*
4. *Caproni-Campini CC-2, flown by Italians on August 27, 1940.*
5. *Japan's first jet fighter, the Kikka, powered by two Ne-20s.*

3.

4.

5.

The Forties...decade of emergence

THE FORTIES

If the decade of the 1930s was a time for the initial budding of gas turbines as a primary source for aircraft power, the ten years beginning in 1940 marked the emergence of jet engines to power airplanes higher, faster and farther.

Military requirements on both sides of the 1939-1945 World War spurred ever-larger efforts to develop turbine technology—at first to improve performance and increase production of the turbosupercharger and later to perfect the jet engine itself. And although piston engine, propeller-driven aircraft were the major strategic factor in the ultimate outcome of the conflict, the Jet Age had already dawned —in 1939…1940…1941…or 1942. It depended upon which side of a world at war you were sitting on.

Famous GE-turbosupercharged World War II aircraft:
1. *Boeing B-29 Superfortress;*
2. *Lockheed P-38 Lightning;*
3. *Consolidated B-24 Liberator;*
4. *Republic P-47 Thunderbolt;*
5. *Boeing B-17 Flying Fortress.*
6. *R.G. Standerwick, Dr. S.A. Moss with Type B turbosupercharger.*

1.

2.

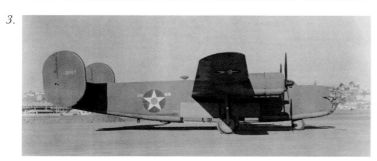

3.

5.

4.

GE gears up for defense production

In 1940, with General Electric turbos on order for the B-17, P-38, and B-24, it became obvious the company must expand research and production capabilities at the Lynn Works.

GE was "tooling up" with people as well as facilities to meet the already apparent defense needs of the Allies—under the Lend-Lease plan—and for what some believed might be a U.S. involvement in the war.

Reginald Standerwick, a man of great dignity and presence (who had provided engineering support for those first Army Air Corps turbos in the early 1920s), was named managing engineer of the Supercharger department. He reported to the company's vice president of engineering, Roy C. Muir, who was headquartered in Schenectady.

Beginning in 1940, Standerwick presided over a personnel buildup in the Lynn Supercharger department that brought together a group of young, eager and enthusiastic managers, engineers, and technicians who would shape the destiny of GE's aircraft engine business for the next three decades. In a few cases, these "young turks" of the early 1940s are still active contributors to the company's progress as it enters the 1980s.

6.

The Lynn engineering staff was also augmented by an influx of experienced gas and steam turbine engineers from Schenectady.

E.S. "Tommy" Thompson, later to be in charge of GE's aircraft gas turbine sales and support activities, came from Schenectady to the Supercharger department to head installation engineering and customer contact.

Dale Streid had moved from Schenectady in the late '30s and was already deeply involved in the propulsion studies under way in the Thomson Lab. He was joined at Lynn by Donald F. "Truly" Warner from the Steam Turbine division. Warner would become a leading player in the drama that was to unfold in the next several years as America entered the Jet Age. Joe Alford and Gene Stoeckly also came from the Schenectady Works during that period—beginning their nearly 40-year careers as preeminent gas turbine engineers, technical advisors and counselors. Floyd Heglund and William Travers were among the 1940 crop of engineering school graduates who would become part of the gathering of "jet pioneers" in the '40s.

One of Gene Stoeckly's first jobs was to design enclosed cells for testing turbosuperchargers. The cells were to simulate flight conditions at altitudes up to 25,000 feet so that turbos could be tested under actual operating conditions. For years afterward there was never any doubt along Boston's North Shore when GE turbos were on test. Huge clouds of steam created by the steam ejectors used to reduce the cell pressure would billow forth into the Massachusetts sky to be diffused by the prevailing ocean winds.

1. Joseph S. Alford.
2. Eugene E. Stoeckly.
3. Donald F. "Truly" Warner.
4. Lynn River Works.

3.

1.

2.

Two new plant sites were selected to supplement Lynn production. The Everett, Massachusetts, plant—still a major engine component facility— was begun in 1940 and went into production by 1941. The Taylor Street plant at Ft. Wayne, Indiana, was added to the growing empire of the Supercharger department. Under the leadership of Harold D. Kelsey, who would later manage the entire aircraft engine operation in the postwar period, Ft. Wayne garnered praise for its high production and low unit costs during the 1941-45 wartime period. At Everett, Claude H. Auger, who would make major contributions to GE's gas turbine progress, was in charge of manufacturing engineering, and he also had responsibility for liaison between the various turbine manufacturing groups.

In addition to its internal expansion, GE augmented production capability by licensing Allis Chalmers in Milwaukee, and Ford Motor Company in Detroit, to produce Type B turbosuperchargers. Arthur Cavanaugh, who provided liaison with the two licensees and the Army Air Corps, began a long career in gas turbines that would ultimately see him in charge of the company's Dayton, Geneva, Switzerland and Oklahoma City, aircraft gas turbine offices.

By mid-1941—some six months before the U.S. entered the war—GE turbosuperchargers were in mass production in Massachusetts, Indiana, Michigan and Wisconsin and were already seeing combat service with Allied air forces under the Lend-Lease program.

4.

THE FORTIES

GE turbine power studies move forward

In the late 1930s, the Army and GE had started exchanging technical papers and bulletins on the subject of gas turbines as a primary source of power. The practice continued through 1940 and early 1941.

At Lynn in early 1940, Dale Streid and Ed Harrison produced one of these papers. It was a study entitled, "Airplane Gas Turbine with Propeller or Jet Propulsion." The study was modified during the course of the year and issued in final form in November with completed curves for various altitudes and pressure ratios for both gas turbine driven propeller and pure jet propulsion.

At Schenectady's Steam Turbine division, development work had been under way since 1936 on a gas turbine powered railroad locomotive. This basic study also included the possibility of gas turbine propulsion for ships. (Steam turbines had been in naval use since the 1920s, generating electricity to power the giant motors that turn ships' propellers, but had not as yet been used for direct drive.)

As an interesting sidelight, some Schenectady engineers considered using a gas turbine to drive an airplane's propeller. Thoughts of engines producing 10,000 horsepower—in contrast to the then current piston engines that could generate up to 5,000 horsepower—were thwarted by the relatively low efficiency of the turbines and compressors of the day.

Because of these continuing gas turbine studies for a variety of land, sea and air transportation applications, GE's Alan Howard, a leader in Schenectady's development work, was invited to the National Advisory Committee for Aeronautics' (NACA) Cleveland laboratories to witness work under way on a new type of compressor. A significant breakthrough in gas turbine technology was about to take place.

Up to that time, all GE gas turbine compressors—and most of the other work in the world, including the Whittle studies in Britain and the already successful von Ohain engine in Germany—had been based on the centrifugal flow compressor principle. In fact, the turbosupercharger was a kind of "mini" jet engine consisting of a centrifugal compressor and a turbine drive, but lacking a combustion system.

1.

2.

3.

1. Glenn B. Warren.
2. Alan Howard.
3. Bruce O. Buckland.

Centrifugal flow compressors whirl the incoming air in a circular casing, compressing it into higher pressure by forcing it to the outside of the casing —not unlike the effect of rapidly swinging a bucket of water in circles without spilling any. But, as the need for higher pressures to achieve greater power became evident, designers recognized that the centrifugal compressor would become larger and larger, the hardware too heavy, and the frontal area of the engine so big that it would become a major obstacle for airplane designers.

In contrast to the centrifugal compressor, the axial flow concept uses a series of blades mounted on a rotating shaft combined with stationary blades mounted in the casing to compress air as it moves straight through an enclosed tube, flowing in the direction of the axis.

The axial flow principle was not new. In fact, Lorin described this concept in his 1908 French patent, and now NACA had built and tested an axial flow compressor in its Cleveland laboratories.

Howard and his GE compatriots, Glenn Warren—to whom Howard then reported—and Bruce Buckland, were convinced this was the answer to the design of the turboprop engine.

As Glenn Warren later recalled, ''We contracted to build and test a four-stage axial flow compressor. We made the blades adjustable and promptly broke them all off on the first stall.''

The early GE work on the axial flow gas turbine, interestingly, was conducted for the U.S. Navy, looking to a powerplant for PT boats. It included a Navy contract to build and test a combustion chamber and a single stage turbine, using shop supply air for power. The compressed air capacity at the Schenectady Works was relatively low at that time and the design engineers feared that if they built and operated a full size test unit, it might shut down the entire plant. So, they scaled down the size of all the components and rigged their own air supply with a large, low-speed motor driving an air compressor.

In one of those ''miracles'' associated with technology advances, an incidental constraint led to a more profound discovery: The components originally planned to power a Navy PT boat—and reduced in size to accommodate the test facilities available—were soon to be used in the development of the gas turbine engine for aircraft.

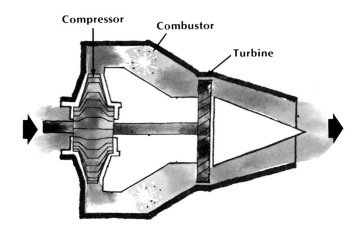

Centrifugal Flow Turbojet Engine

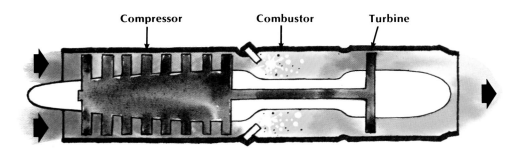

Axial Flow Turbojet Engine

THE FORTIES

1941 is a pivotal year

In January, 1941, the National Academy of Sciences, fully aware of the many gas turbine studies under way in the U.S. and Europe, urged that gas turbines be developed to power ships. The NAS report was an impetus to gas turbine development, but the study also concluded that gas turbines would be impractical for aircraft because they would weigh 13 pounds for every unit of horsepower delivered—in contrast to the current piston engines approaching the production of one horsepower for every pound of weight.

As a result of the NAS report, the three leading U.S. manufacturers of turbines—GE, Allis Chalmers and Westinghouse—had been awarded U.S. Navy contracts to study marine gas turbines. It was under this contract that the Schenectady Steam Turbine division work on the PT boat powerplant was being undertaken.

During the same period U.S. intelligence sources had received scattered information on the German jet engine effort (they did *not* know the He 178 had already flown) and, of course, were aware of the British hardware work.

On February 25, 1941, General H.H. Arnold, Deputy Chief of Staff for Air (who later commanded all U.S. Army Air Forces in World War II and is called "the Father of the United States Air Force"), wrote to Dr. Vannevar Bush, chairman of NACA (and later renowned for his work on the atomic bomb), urging NACA to form a jet research group. At the time, rocket propulsion was linked with jet propulsion and the implication was that the study group was to include that form of aircraft propulsion in its charter.

In March, Dr. Bush created a "Special Committee on Jet Propulsion" within NACA. The committee was headed by Dr. Will Durand, Dr. Moss' Cornell professor and the chairman of NACA during World War I. Dr. Durand, of course, had promoted the development of the turbosupercharger during the 1914-1918 conflict. The committee included representatives from the Army Air Corps, Navy Bureau of Aeronautics, National Bureau of Standards, Johns Hopkins University and Massachusetts Institute of Technology, and from the three U.S. turbine manufacturers—Allis Chalmers, Westinghouse and General Electric. The inclusion of representatives from the companies was significant both in the intended direction of the work of the committee and in the ultimate outcome of aircraft gas turbine work in the U.S.

1.

1. Dr. William F. Durand, NACA chairman during World War I; chairman of NACA special jet propulsion committee in World War II.

2. World's first turboprop, GE TG-100 with Alan Howard, Dr. Chapman Walker, circa 1945.

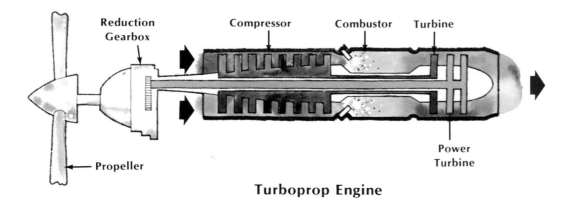

Reduction Gearbox — **Compressor** — **Combustor** — **Turbine** — **Propeller** — **Power Turbine**

Turboprop Engine

General Arnold had specifically requested that the then-leading U.S. manufacturers of aircraft engines *not* be included on the committee. His reason was apparently that they were heavily involved in the wartime military aircraft buildup plus the fact that aircraft gas turbines were unorthodox—entirely different from the piston engines used to power airplanes since the original flight of the Wright brothers in 1903.

In June the three gas turbine manufacturers submitted engine proposals—all based on axial flow compressors. Allis Chalmers' proposal was for a ducted-fan engine (in effect, an encased multi-bladed propeller which served as an added compressor providing extra air); Westinghouse selected a pure turbojet; and GE, basing its proposal on the Schenectady studies, submitted a turboprop.

By July, 1941, NACA had decided to give the three manufacturers an OK to proceed with development work. On July 7, 1941, GE started design in Schenectady of the world's first turboprop engine. In September, the Durand committee recommended that all three projects be carried forward by the U.S. military services. By the following month the Army and Navy had assumed leadership of aircraft engine development and by early 1942 Allis Chalmers and Westinghouse were under contract to the Navy, GE to the Army Air Corps.

An intriguing sidelight to these events of late 1941-early 1942 was that each service had contracted for engines it didn't really want. The Navy was more interested in the GE turboprop, but the Air Corps contracted for it; the Army was more interested in the turbojet and ducted fan, but the Navy became the contracting authority.

The world's first turboprop engine was designated the TG-100 (later the T31). This early development, coupled with the U.S. decision in 1941 to investigate the British Whittle engine, was to set the scene for a major General Electric decision later in the 1940s.

2.

THE FORTIES

A jet engine design comes to the U.S.

Some American military strategists and high level government officials—as well as a segment of the U.S. scientific community—already knew that development of the Whittle engine had been steadily proceeding in England. The W-1X had first been tested in December, 1940, and a modified version —considered suitable for flight—was run in April, 1941. On May 15, 1941, the Gloster E.28/39, with test pilot Gerry Sayer at the controls, flew for the first time. Now, England, too, had entered the Jet Age.

Most of the world believed the British were the *second* to fly a jet propelled aircraft after the Italians' first flight in 1940. In reality they were *third* since the Germans had already flown the He 178 in 1939.

The Italian development had begun in 1933 when Secondo Campini, an Italian engineer, conceived of an interesting approach to jet propulsion. He developed a reciprocating engine driving a compressor inside the fuselage of an airplane (the airframe would become a giant cylinder for the powerplant). The air taken in by this large compressor was exhausted at high velocity at the rear of the aircraft, producing jet thrust.

Campini joined aircraft designer Giavasi Caproni to build the CC-2. It flew for the first time on August 27, 1940, an occasion heralded by the Italians—and the press—as the world's first jet flight.

The Third Reich, already well into Hitler's plan for world conquest, did nothing to counter the story, and kept secret the fact they had already made that historic flight, exactly one year to the day before.

1.

42

1. *Early Whittle engine.*
2. *Gloster E.28/39, powered by a single W-1X.*
3. *R. C. Muir.*

3.

In May, 1941, a few days after the first flight of the Gloster E.28/39—General Arnold was invited by the British Air Ministry to come to England and witness firsthand the successful turbojet engine/airplane combination. The General saw—and was convinced. He returned to Washington with a plan to expedite America's entry into the Jet Age.

The Army Deputy Chief for Air had quickly decided on General Electric as the logical company to carry out the jet engine work because of its heritage of research in turbine technology and its 1917-1941 turbosupercharger experience. Consistent with his request to Dr. Bush earlier in the year that the traditional engine makers not be included on the NACA special committee, General Arnold appeared convinced that the unorthodox nature of this powerplant development might meet with great skepticism from the traditional piston engine manufacturers. Besides, both Pratt & Whitney and Wright were already taxed to capacity with current military work.

Official negotiations were soon begun between the U.S. and British governments for rights to build the Whittle engine in the United States. General Arnold contacted R.C. Muir, GE's vice president of engineering, and requested that a knowledgeable company engineer be dispatched to England. The engineer would work with the Army Air Corps' technical representative in London, Colonel A.J. Lyons, to investigate the challenges of the project.

2.

As it happened, D. Roy Shoults had been sent by the company to England in the spring of 1941—not long before General Arnold's visit to see the E.28/39. He was assigned to support the new customers for the GE supercharged B-17s that were by then providing the British with high altitude bombing capability. Roy Shoults recalled, ''As I went about my turbosupercharger work, I was gradually made aware of the details of the Whittle engine.''

Muir did not have to dispatch anyone from the U.S. The ''knowledgeable engineer'' was already there—and knew of the Whittle project!

Shoults worked with Colonel Lyons. Both became convinced the U.S. should build the engine, but they also believed that Army Air Corps Power Plant Lab people should be consulted. With General Arnold's approval, another knowledgeable engineer—one with considerable experience working with GE turbos in the 1930s—was dispatched from Wright Field, Dayton. Major Donald J. Keirn, later a U.S. Air Force major general deeply involved with aircraft nuclear propulsion, began his association with America's first jet engine.

Events moved quickly in the fall of 1941—three months before the U.S. entry into the conflict. An agreement had been signed by U.S. Secretary of War Henry Stimson and Sir Henry Self of the British Air Commission that would give the U.S. complete details of the Whittle engine—provided that full secrecy was maintained and the number of people involved was held to a minimum.

1. *D. Roy Shoults.*
2. *General H.H. Arnold (right); Lawrence D. Bell, president, Bell Aircraft.*
3. *General Arnold's letter on the ''Whittle matter.''*

1.

2.

Shoults wanted to report his findings to his company, but was prevented by the secrecy order placed on the project. He could not even talk with GE Vice President Muir without the permission of General Arnold. In a letter to Shoults, General Arnold confirmed that the "Whittle matter" could be discussed only with Muir, Alex Stevenson, Sam Puffer and Glenn Warren.

General Arnold convened a top secret meeting in Washington on September 4, 1941. Representing the U.S. Government and the Army Air Corps were Assistant Secretary of War for Air, Robert A. Lovett; Brigadier General Oliver P. Echols, chief of the Army's Materiel Division; Lt. Colonel Benjamin Chidlaw, Materiel's engineering chief; General Carl Spaatz; Major Clarence Irvine; Major Ed Brandt; and, of course, General Arnold. Present for GE were Roy Muir, Dr. Alex Stevenson, Sam Puffer and Roy Shoults.

A small safe sat in the corner of the office where this high powered group of military and industrial officials met. General Arnold turned the combination to the proper settings, opened the safe and took out a sheaf of drawings and reports. After a presentation on the details of the British project by Roy Shoults and Major Brandt, General Arnold said, "Gentlemen, I give you the Whittle engine. Consult all you wish and arrive at any decision you please— just so long as General Electric accepts a contract to build 15 of them."

Stressing the secrecy of the project, General Arnold turned over the papers to the GE representatives. After a brief consultation, notes taken that day by Roy Shoults say, "Mr. Muir assured General Arnold that we would undertake this project and could do it at the River Works [Lynn] without handicapping the turbosupercharger operation."

That historic decision out of the way, the conferees discussed the selection of a "suitable airplane firm to build three airplanes." Bell Aircraft of Buffalo, New York, was selected and its president, Larry Bell, summoned to Washington for a following-day meeting to be briefed and presented with the challenge. Shoults stayed over in Washington to help brief the Bell people on the revolutionary engine/airframe project.

3.

WAR DEPARTMENT
OFFICE OF THE CHIEF OF STAFF
WASHINGTON

August 27, 1941

Mr. D. R. Shoults,
    c/o General Electric Company,
    Schenectady, New York.

Dear Mr. Shoults:

    Confirming our conversation of this morning, you are authorized to discuss the Whittle matter with Mr. Muir, Mr. Stevenson, Mr. Puffer, and Mr. Warren.

    You will inform these four gentlemen of the secret status of the discussions.

               Sincerely,

               H. H. ARNOLD,
               Major General, U. S. A.,
               Deputy Chief of Staff for Air.

Lynn springs into action—secretly

In the face of acknowledged material shortages, the dwindling supply of engineers and skilled craftsmen caused by the war production buildup, and increased turbosupercharger production at Lynn, Muir had committed the company to build and test the first U.S. jet engine in six months.

A handpicked team of Lynn River Works gas turbine experts, headed by Truly Warner, was assembled and galvanized into action—with full recognition of what seemed to be an impossible deadline.

Although much of the work was going to depend on supercharger engineering and production facilities, turbosupercharger employees were not allowed access to the newly designated "top secret" engineering and drafting building and the special test cell being prepared for the buildup. When parts had to be manufactured for the secret project they were designated as "Type I supercharger components." Many a Lynn worker secretly believed he was "in the know" about the company's classified project to build a "powerful, giant turbosupercharger."

Supercharger department managers Reginald Standerwick and Sam Puffer were, of course, an integral part of the team and provided all of the technical and manufacturing support for the top secret effort. Any employee new to the project—even if transferred from another GE operation—had to be personally screened by corporate engineering Vice President Muir. Even the Army Air Corps plant representative assigned to the River Works for supercharger business was prohibited from entering the classified area. To use the terminology of a later day, no one—including his superiors—considered he had a critical "need to know."

1.

Tension mounted as the British drawings were carefully examined and modified from English to American specifications, and individual parts were ordered into almost handcrafted manufacture. Under the contract for the engines—a simple one-sentence document that called for the delivery of 15 Type I (pronounced "eye," not "one") superchargers—GE had agreed to produce the engines in accordance with the original British specifications. It soon became apparent, however, that the drawings were incomplete in some very important aspects—the engine control system, for example—and many design features that years of GE steam and gas turbine experience had demonstrated to be impractical had to be modified.

Not long after the initiation of the project, Warner decided the chances for success would be improved if an actual Whittle engine could be studied. An official request was expedited and, in England, an early test model, the W-1X, was crated for shipment to Lynn. Accompanied by Major Keirn, who defied all of the normal channels, cut corners and used his "top secret" orders from General Arnold whenever he was really pushed into a corner, the W-1X arrived in Lynn on October 4 by way of Bolling Field, Washington, D.C. There U.S. customs officials insisted they had to examine the contents of the crate and Keirn just as strongly insisted they could not. Keirn finally compromised by permitting a customs official to "count" the number of crates in the shipment; face was saved and the U.S. jet engine program proceeded.

In addition to Keirn, three British technicians had accompanied the engine. The "man-to-man" communications proved extremely helpful during the next several months as ideas, problems and past experiences were shared and obstacles overcome.

1. *Jet pioneers await early tests: included are Lynn's Gus Berg (second from left); Truly Warner (center); NACA's Dr. Durand (second from right).*

2. *America's first turbojet, General Electric I-A.*

2.

First engine test

In early 1942 all of the planning, drawings, engineering and manufacturing began to come together and the first engine was assembled for test. Installed in the special test cell—affectionately named "Fort Knox" by the Type I crew in recognition of its 18-inch thick walls—the first engine ran on March 18. But, it stalled well below full speed. The British had encountered the same problem. Calling on turbosupercharger experience, GE engineers returned to the drawing board and modified key parts of the engine.

Exactly one month later—April 18, 1942—the still preserved test log recorded historic words: "Everybody working to finish Type I so that it could go in Fort Knox....We did a great deal of checking before attempting to start; a great deal of trifling troubles were found and remedied—but after many attempts Type I RAN."

At the top of the log sheet—in bold letters and with heavy underscoring—was printed: "Type I runs at 11:05 p.m. Operator-D. Warner." Truly Warner had been given the ultimate honor: *operating the first jet engine in the United States.*

At the bottom of the log sheet one sentence quietly summed up the exhilaration felt on that spring day in Lynn, Massachusetts: "Everyone worked like beavers but all felt well repaid."

2.

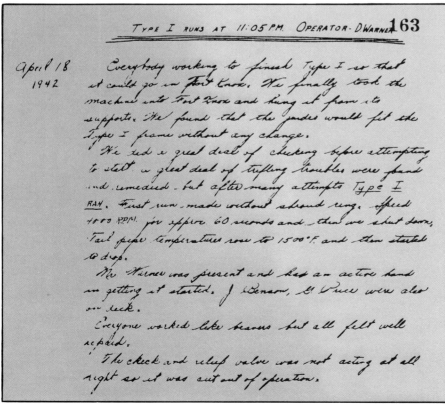

1.

1. Log sheet, April 18, 1942, first U.S. jet engine tested.
2. The door to "Fort Knox."
3. GE I-16 on outdoor test.

In June, 1942, Frank Whittle arrived in the U.S. to provide advice and counsel as the engines scheduled for installation in the Bell airplane were prepared for the first flight. Traveling under an assumed name—the one chosen was Frank Whitley, which hardly seemed designed to fool any foreign spy—Whittle at first stayed in a Boston hotel until this arrangement was deemed too risky. He was moved to the Marblehead, Massachusetts, home of Reginald Standerwick, under the same Whitley guise. Although he stayed for some weeks, traveling back and forth between Marblehead and the River Works, it wasn't until many months later that Standerwick's wife—and others who came into regular contact with "Whitley"—learned who the important house guest had been. Apparently the ruse had worked.

With successful bench tests complete, the flight engines were shipped to Bell at Buffalo for mating with the airframe. But, before the historic first flight was to take place, one major obstacle remained: transporting the engines and propeller-less airplane all the way across the country to the California desert, the site selected for the tests—in secrecy and unharmed.

Among many logistics problems confronting the designers as they prepared their valuable cargo for the trip was what to do about protecting the engines' ball bearings and shafts which had been machined to extremely fine tolerances; the constant jolting and bumping encountered on a long rail trip would almost certainly damage them.

3.

Standerwick, Warner and Keirn discussed the problem and decided the only solution was to "run" the engines as they traveled across the U.S.—turning the shaft continuously by means of a small gas-driven air compressor. Much to the surprise of the three GE installation engineers who had supervised the mating of the engines and the airframe—Frank Burnham, Angus McEachern and Ted Rogers—they discovered they had "volunteered" to accompany the shipment. The only problem was that the entourage and their top secret cargo would travel in a freight car and provisions had not been made for human comforts.

The three-man team did emergency provisioning: mattresses, blankets, canned food. Paired with a group of five U.S. Army security guards, the "gypsies" and their valuable cargo began their odyssey. They said later that the trip was definitely not the way to "see the U.S.A." In Kansas City, Burnham—assured that the stopped train would not leave for 20 minutes—dashed out for fresh rations. Returning to the rail yard with provisions for the next leg, he couldn't find the train. It had left. In near-Hollywood-like fashion, he caught the next express coming through the yards and intercepted the high priority freight somewhere in Kansas. Since he carried all the pooled funds, the jet pioneers gave Burnham a warm welcome and made sure he stayed safely aboard thereafter.

4.

2.

1. *Frank Burnham, Ed Tritle, Roy Shoults, Ted Rogers, Angus McEachern at Muroc, 1942.*

2. *The "intrepid three" return: McEachern, Rogers, Burnham, at Muroc (Edwards AFB), 1967.*

3. *P-59 with dummy propeller.*

4. *Bell P-59.*

3.

First flight

In mid-September the entourage arrived at Muroc Dry Lake, California (later to become famous as Edwards Air Force Base). The remote site had been chosen for the historic flight because of its excellent weather conditions and the expanse of dry lake bed that provided miles of unencumbered takeoff and, more to the point, landing space.

The secrecy of the historic mission was carefully maintained. In order to "fool" the experienced aviators who frequented the area, a dummy wooden propeller was attached to the nose of the P-59, giving it the appearance of a conventional, single piston engine powered fighter.

After around-the-clock preparations by the Army Air Corps/Bell/GE team, on September 29 Bell chief test pilot Bob Stanley was ready for the first taxi tests. Late in the afternoon, with Larry Bell, Truly Warner and Roy Shoults pacing back and forth in front of the hangar like expectant fathers, Stanley taxied the airplane, designated the XP-59A Airacomet, and actually lifted it a few feet off the runway. But, more-than-routine checking, adjustments, fine tuning and consultations would take place over the next several days before everyone was satisfied.

On October 2, 1942, all agreed the historic day had arrived. Ted Rogers, one of GE's "intrepid three" freight car travelers and later a veteran Lynn engineer and manufacturing manager, recalled the drama: *"...we worked until 3:30 a.m. (the morning of the flight)...this was the day! Stanley climbed into the cockpit... a brief wave...and he was off, taxiing to the far end of the field. He turned at the end of his taxi run and ran both engines alternately to maximum speed...a momentary pause while the pilot released the brakes... the jets began to take hold...the plane rolled ever so slowly at first...with us mentally pushing it on...soon began to pick up speed...just opposite us it lifted gently into the air...continued straight away, gaining altitude...past the end of the field...banked and crossed directly over our heads...what a strange feeling... dead silence as it passed directly overhead...then a low rumbling roar like a blow torch...and it was gone, leaving a smell of kerosene in the air...after about ten minutes of low level flight, Bob landed..."*

October 2, 1942—only 13 months after General Arnold's historic Washington meeting—America had entered the Jet Age.

THE FORTIES

The power grows

By the time of the first jet flight, the GE Type I engine had been designated the I-A. It was rated at 1,250 pounds of thrust. After flight tests began, it quickly became apparent that more powerful engines would significantly increase the performance of the airplane—particularly the planned operational combat fighter version.

Almost immediately the Lynn team began studies to increase the thrust output of the I-A. The cadre of GE turbine pioneers—by now the combined turbosupercharger and jet engine teams—had been augmented by another key individual. Dr. Sanford Moss, who had retired from the company in 1938, came back as a consultant to aid the frenzied wartime effort. Dr. Moss provided technical assistance throughout the war years as both GE superchargers and jet engines became more powerful, larger and more complex.

In 1941 Dr. Moss became the first General Electric engineer to receive aviation's coveted Collier Trophy when he was presented the 1940 award for "outstanding success in high altitude flying by the development of the turbosupercharger." Dr. Moss, who held 46 patents on superchargers, compressors and other mechanical devices, was recognized on his 70th birthday in 1942 with this message from the U.S. Army Air Corps' commander, General Hap Arnold: "Your contribution of the airplane supercharger and turbosupercharger is outstanding in the science of aeronautics." Dr. Moss died in 1946.

Although generally patterned after the original I-A, engines with higher thrust ratings (1,400, 1,600 and 2,000 pounds of thrust) were designed that reflected more advanced GE technologies in compressor design and employed higher temperature metals already developed for turbosuperchargers. The engine designations were derived from their thrust ratings. The I-14 (1,400 pounds of thrust) used fewer turbine blades and included a new combustion liner developed by A.J. "Tony" Nerad of GE's Schenectady Research Laboratory, who had also designed the combustor for the TG-100 turboprop about the same time.

Production of a more powerful engine for an advanced XP-59 centered on the I-16, whose design had begun in January, 1943. Averaging 1,650 pounds of thrust with a 1,600 pound guarantee, two I-16s flew to an altitude of 46,700 feet in a fully armed P-59 in July, 1943.

A small quantity of I-14s were built. The relatively higher power I-20 was never put into production because by then military requirements called for significant thrust increases. Of the original derivatives from the Whittle design, 30 I-As and 241 I-16s were eventually delivered to the Army Air Force.

In early 1943 intelligence reports from Europe confirmed that the Germans had flown not only the He 178, but another pure jet as well—the Messerschmidt Me 262. British efforts were moving ahead, but the pace was slow. A twin-jet fighter had not yet flown in England and, although the U.S. Airacomet had demonstrated significant performance improvements, it was not as fast as hoped for and the stability of the airplane as a gun platform in aerial combat was questionable.

The U.S. Army Air Force strategists called for American jets capable of leapfrogging any Axis developments. Speed—as much as 500 miles per hour—was the primary criterion.

1.

Speed meant significantly more powerful engines. The Air Force asked GE to consider developing a 4,000 pound thrust engine—more powerful than any aircraft engine then in existence. The company, making one of its most significant aviation business decisions up to that time, elected to proceed with the development of not one, but *two*, aircraft gas turbines in the 4,000 pound thrust class.

Concurrent with the engine development, the AAF turned to Lockheed Aircraft in Burbank, California, because of their work with the record-setting P-38 Lightning. A Lockheed team under the leadership of the famed C.L. "Kelly" Johnson, who had been responsible for the P-38 design, began work on a new airplane designated the XP-80 Shooting Star.

Recognizing that engine development would almost certainly take longer than the airframe, the AAF made arrangements with the British to obtain the deHavilland Goblin engine for initial XP-80 flight testing. But, operating under complete wartime secrecy, AAF officials knew that the more powerful GE engine would eventually provide XP-80 propulsion—although they had not as yet informed the Lockheed team.

In June, 1943, GE began development of the I-40 (later designated the J33) under the leadership of Dale Streid. The first engine went on test in January, 1944. Within a month the I-40 had produced 4,200 pounds of thrust—believed to be the highest power ever achieved up to that time from a jet engine. The engines were ready for the Shooting Star.

Although the XP-80 had already flown with the British engine, the first flight with the I-40 powerplant took place on June 10, 1944—only one year after the start of engine development. The reengined XP-80—with the I-40 providing 40 percent more thrust than the Goblin—performed up to all expectations. The U.S. had the fastest, highest flying, most powerful fighter in the world. The P-80 went on to become the first U.S. Army Air Force operational jet and, in 1947, broke the world's speed record—then held by a British Gloster Meteor IV— by flying at 620 miles per hour.

2.

3.

1. Lockheed XP-80 Shooting Star, powered by J33.
2. A.J. Nerad.
3. R.G. Standerwick with I-40.

THE FORTIES

The I-40 makes a mark—and moves on

In addition to having the distinction of being the first U.S.-designed operational jet engine, the I-40/J33 also became the proving ground for a number of the "young turks" who had moved into GE's Supercharger department in early 1940—it provided an opportunity to apply theories and technical knowledge under realistic "game" conditions.

Members of the Dale Streid-directed I-40 team included men who would become the leaders of GE's progress in aircraft gas turbines for the next quarter-century. Neil Burgess, who had reported to the Supercharger department in July, 1941, was part of the I-40 project, and would become a key figure in the development of the J47 and J79 engines as well as in the company's entry into civil aviation. Others included Bert Sells, Dick Novak, Earl Auyer and Len Heurlin. Another young engineer destined to leave his mark on many GE engines of the future, Martin C. Hemsworth, helped design a special vacuum test pit for I-40 turbine discs. He would go on to bigger projects, including the world's largest turbofan engine.

1.

The I-40 also provided a reverse flow in the Anglo-American relations that had blossomed as a result of jet engine developments. In May, 1944, a delegation of distinguished British engineers and scientists spent several days in Lynn and Schenectady reviewing GE gas turbine progress and exchanging views. The high point of the meetings came when GE unveiled a full-size cutaway of the I-40 engine, revealing its 4,000 pound thrust output. The British delegation had not seriously envisioned an engine of that power.

Dr. Stanley Hooker of Rolls Royce carefully studied the drawings and the performance specifications and announced, "Now I've seen that it can be done, I'm going back home, pull up my socks, and go to work!" The impetus had been provided. Rolls Royce developed the Nene, similar in size and installation arrangements to the I-40, but with a number of significant improvements.

As the I-40/J33 took on added significance in the strategy of wartime, the Air Force became concerned about GE's production capacity at Lynn. They wanted quantity production quickly. The first step was to take over a GE naval turbine plant in Syracuse, New York, and ultimately to license the production of J33 engines to the Allison division of General Motors at Indianapolis. GE produced 300 J33s by war's end and Allison ultimately built thousands of the GE-designed engine.

2.

Axial flow compressor engines developed in parallel

Secrecy was the order of the day in Schenectady as well as in Lynn. Under the same conditions that prevailed at the River Works, the axial flow turbo-prop TG-100/T31 (whose design had started in July, 1941) was successfully ground tested for the first time on May 15, 1943. The engine produced 1,200 horsepower and weighed 800 pounds. Glenn Warren and Alan Howard had moved the project along rapidly, benefitting from the Anglo/American technology exchange.

Warren said, "One of the most important contributions which we got [from the British efforts], in my judgement, was the concept of the 'multiple combustion cans.' " This concept helped simplify the problem of the combustion of gases used to turn the turbine. Tony Nerad applied this concept to the Research Laboratory's combustion work, aided by Don Berkey, a young engineer who was to become one of the guiding technical geniuses of the aircraft engine business in the decades ahead. When improved combustors were needed for advanced engines, they were ready.

As they proceeded with development of the turbo-prop TG-100, the Schenectady Steam Turbine division technicians believed they could also build an axial flow compressor turbojet. Design work was begun in 1943 on the engine; the practical requirement was provided when the Air Force expressed the need for a 4,000 pound thrust engine. As a result, the company decided to propose not only the centrifugal flow I-40/J33 but the axial flow TG-180 (later designated the J35) as well.

That decision had not come easily. In Schenectady and Lynn, technical and management meetings had gone on for months as the company pondered the wisdom of a divided effort. Finally, a major conclusion was reached that was to affect GE's aircraft gas turbine progress for many years to come. Although the I-40 was the engine most likely to be ready for wartime service (since it was based on already demonstrated concepts), Roy Muir and his technical advisors reasoned that the axial flow TG-180 had longer term potential because of its advanced design. The decision was made: meet short and long term needs—propose both.

The Air Force, exhibiting the same wisdom, ordered both engines into development.

1. *Bert Sells.*
2. *Earl Auyer.*
3. *TG-180/J35.*

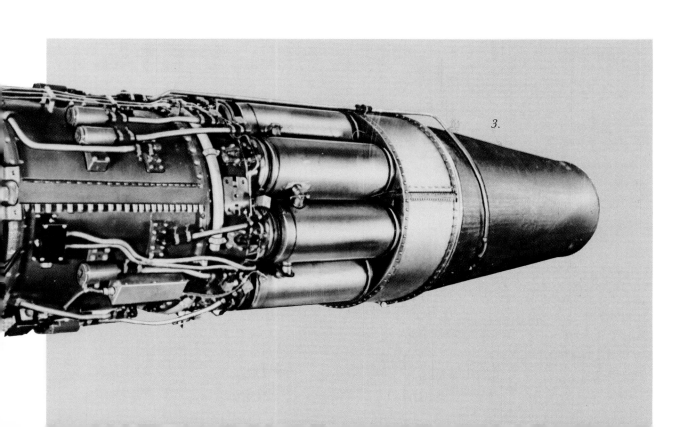

THE FORTIES

The TG-180 first went to test on April 21, 1944—less than a year after the start of design. But with the I-40/J33 already successfully installed in the Lockheed XP-80—and promptly confirming the company's 1943 reasoning—work on the TG-180/J35 proceeded more slowly. The engine was not flight tested until February, 1946, in a Republic XP-84. The company eventually produced 140 of the J35s although—at Air Force direction—prime production responsibility for J35s was transferred to the Chevrolet Motor Division of General Motors in Tonawanda, New York, before the war ended. In 1947—after Chevrolet began postwar automobile production—J35 production was shifted to Allison, which had already been building the GE J33.

The I-40/J33 achieved its greatest fame in the Lockheed P-80 but also powered a ''big brother'' of the P-59, the Bell XP-83. Further confirming the wisdom of the GE management decision, the TG-180/J35 was used in the original twin-jet Northrop F-89 interceptor, the eight-engine Northrop XB-49 Flying Wing, the six-jet Martin XB-48 medium bomber, the Douglas D-558 Skystreak research aircraft (which captured the world speed mark at 650 miles per hour in 1947), the original Republic XP-84 Thunderjet, the four-engine Consolidated Vultee XB-46 medium bomber, and the Hughes XH-17 crane helicopter. The J35 also powered the first versions of the Boeing six-jet XB-47 medium bomber (the plane that crossed the U.S. in three hours and forty-six minutes in 1949—ten years before civil jetliners would accomplish the same feat with engines 150 percent more powerful).

J35-powered aircraft:
1. *Northrop XB-49 Flying Wing;*
2. *Douglas D-558 Skystreak;*
3. *Republic XP-84 Thunderjet;*
4. *Martin XB-48 medium bomber;*
5. *Hughes XH-17 crane helicopter.*

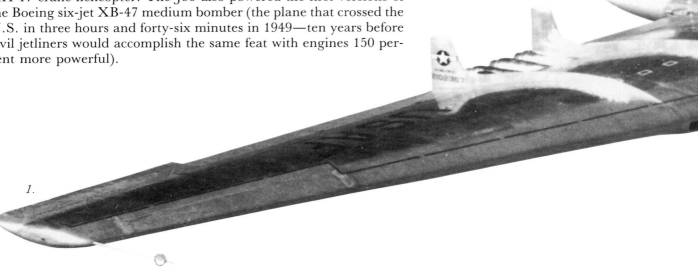

1.

2.

3.

War's end brings realignment

As with all wars in modern history, the end of World War II brought gigantic celebrations by the victors, planning for the restoration and rehabilitation of the conquered—and an almost immediate rollback of development and production of defense work. In the U.S., both government and industry quickly sought a return to a peacetime economy.

Gas turbine technology had played a major strategic role in the ultimate allied victory—but in the form of turbosuperchargers, not jet engines. The high altitude bombing of German industry and the strikes at the Japanese homeland had brought the 1939-1945 war to a swifter conclusion. General Billy Mitchell's convictions of the 1920s had been proved correct. Although the jet powered fighters rushed into development and production by both the Allied and Axis powers during the early 1940s essentially had had no effect on the outcome of the conflict, the period of World War II had marked the emergence of the jet engine as the primary source of aircraft power. The major question facing military planners, the now-gargantuan aviation industry and, eventually, civil aviation was: where do we go from here?

In a period of typical postwar regrouping, the U.S. Army Air Force's answer was: economize and consolidate.

The AAF could not afford two sources for J33 production. GE's Syracuse engine plant was shut down and, although a few J33s were still being produced at Lynn, mass production was centralized with Allison. Chevrolet no longer wanted to produce J35s and this engine, too, was turned over to Allison. Ironically, each of these GE-designed engines was to be mass-produced by another company and become significant competition for General Electric in the next few years.

4.

5.

Within General Electric, work was to continue on development of the TG-180/J35 for a wide variety of applications. But the Schenectady-designed engine was transferred to Lynn when a company decision was made that the Steam Turbine division would concentrate on its traditional land and sea applications for turbines and all aviation activities would be centralized at the River Works.

On July 31, 1945 the Lynn Supercharger department went out of existence and in its place was created the Aircraft Gas Turbine division.

Harold D. Kelsey, who had demonstrated management acumen directing the high volume/low cost supercharger production at Fort Wayne during the war, was named managing engineer of the new division in January, 1946. From then until his transfer to Schenectady in 1949, Kelsey was to face the staunch resistance of skeptics who believed these new jet engines provided nothing but high risk and potential disaster for the company. But, during that same period, Kelsey would make and oversee decisions that set General Electric on a course it would follow for the next several decades—assuring jet engine technology advancement and business continuity.

Reflecting on his role in later years, Kelsey said, ''My biggest contribution was to get General Electric into engine production...I made the decision to drop centrifugal engines and concentrate on the axial flow type.'' Both those achievements had faced major opposition before they became reality.

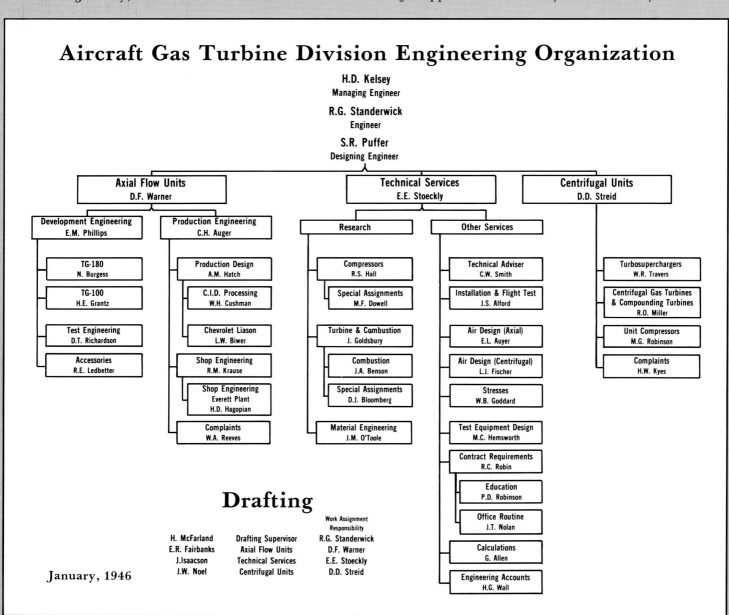

Aircraft Gas Turbine Division Engineering Organization

H.D. Kelsey — Managing Engineer
R.G. Standerwick — Engineer
S.R. Puffer — Designing Engineer

Axial Flow Units — D.F. Warner
- **Development Engineering** — E.M. Phillips
  - TG-180 — N. Burgess
  - TG-100 — H.E. Grantz
  - Test Engineering — D.T. Richardson
  - Accessories — R.E. Ledbetter
- **Production Engineering** — C.H. Auger
  - Production Design — A.M. Hatch
  - C.I.D. Processing — W.H. Cushman
  - Chevrolet Liason — L.W. Biwer
  - Shop Engineering — R.M. Krause
  - Shop Engineering Everett Plant — H.D. Hagopian
  - Complaints — W.A. Reeves

Technical Services — E.E. Stoeckly
- **Research**
  - Compressors — R.S. Hall
  - Special Assignments — M.F. Dowell
  - Turbine & Combustion — J. Goldsbury
  - Combustion — J.A. Benson
  - Special Assignments — D.J. Bloomberg
  - Material Engineering — J.M. O'Toole
- **Other Services**
  - Technical Adviser — C.W. Smith
  - Installation & Flight Test — J.S. Alford
  - Air Design (Axial) — E.L. Auyer
  - Air Design (Centrifugal) — L.J. Fischer
  - Stresses — W.B. Goddard
  - Test Equipment Design — M.C. Hemsworth
  - Contract Requirements — R.C. Robin
  - Education — P.D. Robinson
  - Office Routine — J.T. Nolan
  - Calculations — G. Allen
  - Engineering Accounts — H.G. Wall

Centrifugal Units — D.D. Streid
- Turbosuperchargers — W.R. Travers
- Centrifugal Gas Turbines & Compounding Turbines — R.O. Miller
- Unit Compressors — M.G. Robinson
- Complaints — H.W. Kyes

Drafting

		Work Assignment Responsibility
H. McFarland	Drafting Supervisor	R.G. Standerwick
E.R. Fairbanks	Axial Flow Units	D.F. Warner
J. Isaacson	Technical Services	E.E. Stoeckly
J.W. Noel	Centrifugal Units	D.D. Streid

January, 1946

Postwar challenges

Kelsey and his newly-formed staff promptly developed a postwar business plan for General Electric in the aircraft engine business. A major element of the plan—recognizing the loss of GE's two major engines, the J33 and J35, to another manufacturer—was the development of a more powerful, more fuel efficient engine to be produced by the company at a rate comparable with Allison J33/J35 production.

Kelsey knew that technical development capabilities were already in place in what had by then become one of the most experienced aircraft gas turbine teams in the world. The experience with turbosuperchargers in the '20s, '30s, and '40s and with jet engines during the war years had created the cadre. But it was also evident that production capabilities—plant and equipment—were less than adequate for the ambitious program conceived by the new division staff.

Moreover, there was divisiveness within the Aircraft Gas Turbine division. Some of the most competent technical veterans, who had persevered with the turbosupercharger through years of resistance, strongly favored continuation of the centrifugal flow compressor concept. It was a known quantity; the successful initial GE engines were centrifugal; most other engines then extant had centrifugal compressors. The evidence was there.

Other equally experienced veterans, including Glenn Warren and many on the engineering staff in the Schenectady Research Lab and Steam Turbine division, provided even more convincing evidence. With axial flow compressors, higher pressure ratios and thus more power and growth potential were possible; the frontal area of axial flow engines could be reduced significantly, minimizing aerodynamic problems for aircraft designers; smaller, lighter engines could be designed—in contrast to the greater size and weight characteristics of the centrifugal flow engines.

The decision was made. The Lynn team immediately went to work on the design of a new 5,000 pound thrust axial flow engine—within the basic frame size of the J35 and with greatly improved fuel economy.

Harold D. Kelsey.

The engine, designated the TG-190, was proposed to the Air Force. The presentation included a production rate comparable to Allison's on the J35. The Air Force accepted the proposal. A contract was signed and the company began work on what was to become the most-produced jet engine in history—the J47.

The Air Force decision was one hurdle overcome. Adequate production capability was another yet to be faced. Kelsey and his staff, in two full days of presentations to the company's top management in Schenectady, provided all the details of their business plan—and their capital investment requirements. One element of the plan—the market forecast—predicted a GE aircraft engine business of $35 million by 1950. (J47 production by 1950 would make that projection low by a factor of 10.)

Because of understandable postwar conservatism and a desire for the company to return to commercial projects (jet engines for civil transports were then only a figment in the imagination of a few visionaries), the division received substantially less capital appropriation than requested. But the new engine program was under way—albeit with a reduced budget—and a start could be made on production capabilities. Another hurdle had been overcome.

Large portions of the Lynn River Works, which also housed other GE manufacturing and development facilities, were converted to jet engine production. The Everett plant, which had been producing superchargers since 1941, began to manufacture jet engine components.

1.

The J47 design challenge

The J47 Project was formed on March 19, 1946, with Neil Burgess, who had served on the I-40 team and was the TG-180 engineering manager, in charge. Using TG-180/J35 experience, the J47 team envisioned an engine with the same frame size but with a modified compressor and turbine and an improved lubrication system; it would be capable of producing 5,000 pounds of thrust. That meant lower weight components—a factor that provided some real challenges and near-disasters during the development cycle. But the engineering team, including men who would continue as GE technology leaders for years to come (Elmir Paulson, Earl Auyer, Ed Ledbetter, Jerry Pederson, R.L. "Nick" Carter), overcame the challenges and by the summer of 1948, J47 engines began to roll off Lynn production lines. Seasoned gas turbine veterans Joe Alford and Gene Stoeckly provided needed counsel for the young team.

Demonstrating that management in its infinite wisdom frequently produces positive results from what, at the time, seem like negative actions was the creation of a Lynn compressor test facility. The sharply reduced capital expenditure budget granted the embryonic division by company executives meant a new compressor test chamber that, in the opinion of River Works gas turbine experts was entirely too small for what they envisioned as the requirement for future engine development.

1. *Neil Burgess and Ray Small (top), Harry Truscott and Ed Ledbetter (bottom) with turbosupercharger impellers.*

2. *TG-190/J47 turbojet engine.*

3. *E.S. Thompson, Carl Salmonsen, Neil Burgess with J47.*

3.

Gene Stoeckly, then in charge of technical services including test facilities, looked for alternative ways to achieve the original objective. He convinced the U.S. Navy to bail to GE—for $1 per year—a new steam turbine that had been destined for a now-cancelled destroyer. Stoeckley knew the turbine would provide that necessary power. (The original requirement had been for a 30,000 horsepower drive to test engines with compressor airflow up to 450 pounds per second.) He made certain the other test components were ''large enough'' to match the destroyer turbine—and, of course, to provide the compressor test conditions everyone at Lynn considered necessary. The facility was built. Although the reduced appropriation was overrun by nearly $500,000—Stoeckly later recalled, ''I never came so close to getting fired in my career''—the long term benefit to the company was almost immeasurable.

The Lynn compressor test facility not only provided the company with capabilities to develop compressors up to and including today's more than 50,000 pound thrust high bypass turbofan engines, it was also the platform on which a young German engineer first demonstrated his technical and mechanical prowess.

Gerhard Neumann, later to shape GE's aircraft engine growth in the 1960s and 1970s as vice president and group executive of the Aircraft Engine Group, was credited with overcoming the initial technical difficulties of the compressor test facility and making it a major contributing factor in engine development.

Neumann had joined General Electric in 1948 under unique circumstances. (One of Neumann's trademarks during his long aviation career was the *creation* of ''unique circumstances.'')

During a 10,000 mile jeep trip from Hong Kong to the Middle East in 1947-48—an odyssey shared with his wife, Clarice, and their Airedale, ''Mr. Chips''—the Neumanns stopped in Tehran, Iran. Realizing he would need a job when he returned to the States, Neumann decided to write to General Electric because he knew of the company's work on jet engines. In Tehran without access to U.S. directories, Neumann's immediate problem was where to send the letter.

Mrs. Neumann, a Connecticut native, recalled the company's Bridgeport facility and his letter of application for work at GE was addressed there—with a request to forward it to the proper place.

When Neumann returned to the U.S. in early 1948, he called the Bridgeport plant. Because of his rather unorthodox approach (the letter from Tehran with the ''beautiful stamps''), they remembered him. His application had been forwarded to the Lynn plant.

At Lynn, Neumann was interviewed by a bevy of veteran GE gas turbine engineers. Truly Warner, Gene Stoeckly and Joe Alford were impressed.

Neumann joined GE the next day, working for Sam Puffer and Neil Burgess.

1.

2.

3.

J47 success necessitates further expansion

By the summer of 1948, production J47 engines were coming off the end of the Lynn manufacturing lines. Neil Burgess, Ray Small and a team of dedicated applications engineers had succeeded in having the J47 selected as the powerplant for most of the new first-line military aircraft being designed. The engine provided power for: North American/ USAF F-86 and USN FJ-1 and FJ-2 fighters; Consolidated Vultee/USAF B-46 medium bomber and B-36 long range bomber; Martin/USAF B-51 attack bomber; Northrop/USAF YB-49 Flying Wing; and the Boeing/USAF B-47 Stratojet. The engine had first been flight tested in a Republic/USAF XP-84 Thunderjet.

It was obvious Lynn production capacity must be expanded. But, even with maximum Lynn production, the company concluded it could not meet J47 engine commitments.

A study was initiated to find another plant site. After extensive research, what was considered an ideal location was selected. The U.S. government owned a large facility in Lockland, Ohio (near Cincinnati), that had been built during World War II to produce Wright Aeronautical piston engines.

When originally constructed in the early 1940s, one building of the Wright plant was the largest structure "under roof" in the world. At the formal dedication ceremonies of the plant, the guest of honor was Orville Wright. By then in his 70s, but still retaining the curiosity of an inventor and pilot, Mr. Wright wandered off to investigate the nooks and crannies of the huge engine development and production complex. Came the appointed hour for the ceremonies to begin and the officials discovered they had "lost" Orville Wright. The opening was delayed while Wright Aeronautical officials sent out scouting parties to find their missing honor guest. He was finally located and the plant was dedicated. The complex was so large even one of aviation's greatest pioneers could get lost in its caverns.

1. *Clarice Neumann with jeep at Burma/India border.*
2. *"Mr. Chips."*
3. *Jeep in mountains of Afghanistan.*
4. *Lynn compressor test facility.*

4.

1.

2.

3.

J47-powered aircraft:
1. *North American F-86 Sabrejet;*
2. *Republic XF-91;*
3. *North American B-45 Tornado;*
4. *North American FJ-2 Fury;*
5. *Chase XC-123;*
6. *Martin XB-51;*
7. *Boeing KC-97 (Boost Power);*
8. *Boeing RB/B-47 Stratojet;*
9. *Consolidated Vultee B-36 (Boost Power).*

5.

6.

7.

8.

9.

THE FORTIES

Although a part of the plant was leased out, large portions of it were immediately available; it already had 40 engine test cells; the USAF supported the decision; and it was both convenient to a major metropolitan center and close to USAF's Power Plant Laboratory at Wright Field, Dayton.

The massive logistics problems of moving personnel and equipment and renovating a plant that had been closed for nearly three years were attacked. Marty Hemsworth had the task of creating 14 bigger and more capable jet engine test cells out of the 40 existing piston engine cells. Ken Houseman, one of Lynn's maufacturing leaders, was transferred to Lockland as plant manager. Paul Nichols organized a nationwide network of subcontractors for J47 parts. In the midst of all the reconstruction and renovation, J47 engine production was already in progress.

An engineering staff of 150 had been moved from Lynn, and design and production engineering responsibility for certain models of the J47 had been shifted to Lockland. Two GE supercharger veterans —Claude Auger, who had first joined the company in 1921 on turbos, and Bill Travers, whose turbine experience dated to 1940—were in charge of the engineering operation.

On February 28, 1949, the GE Lockland plant was formally opened. The dedication was marked by a milestone event. The first Lockland-built J47 engine was delivered to the U.S. Air Force "...almost two months ahead of the mobilization schedule which we had set for it," according to Lt. General E.W. Rawlings, then chief of the USAF Materiel Command.

By the end of 1949, Lynn and Lockland J47 production had reached a rate of 200 engines per month at each plant.

The final year of the decade of the 1940s not only brought to a close the most eventful ten years in GE's aircraft gas turbine history, it also marked the beginning of another era of strong growth in the company's progress toward jet engine leadership.

On November 18, 1949, Cramer W. "Jim" LaPierre—who had been assistant engineer at GE's General Engineering Laboratory and most recently vice president of American Machine and Foundry —was named vice president and general manager of General Electric's Aircraft Gas Turbine division.

1.

The decade of emergence

During the momentous decade of the 1940s, World War II had spurred rapid development of the turbine engine in the United States, Britain, Germany, Italy and Japan. But, as might be expected, the end of the world conflict had seen the greatest strides made in the U.S. and England. During the decade an intense, but mutually respectful, technological rivalry developed between the two powers for what eventually would become the domination of world aviation.

The U.S. had lagged behind—for a variety of reasons—in the early development of aircraft jet engine technology. But the 1940s, particularly during the intensity of the war years, was the time during which the American entries in the race demonstrated their ability to produce an extra "kick" as the contest unfolded.

1. Lockland plant test cells.
2. Eighty-seven skills and 8,859 parts result in J47 engine.

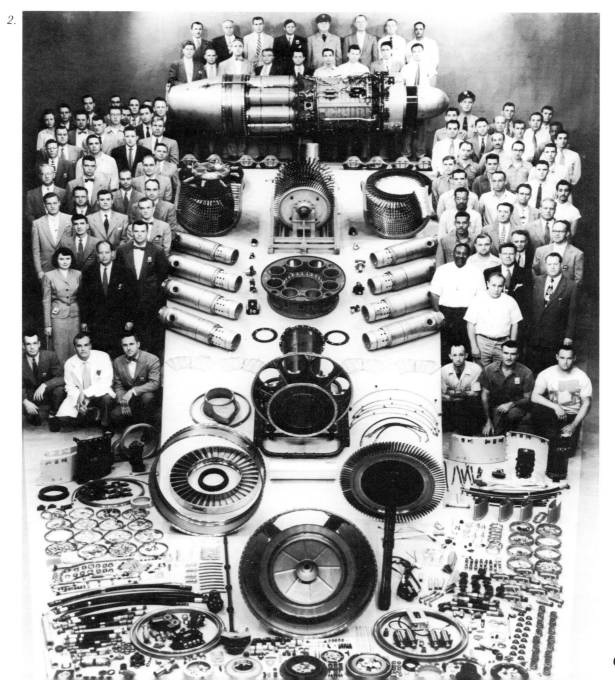

2.

The Fifties...decade of expansion

"There's one thing about GE's engine business—and that is that it is going to be big!"

These prophetic words were uttered by a man in a position to foresee—and affect—the future of General Electric's aircraft engine business. When Cramer W. "Jim" LaPierre made his pronouncement, he had been vice president and general manager of the company's Aircraft Gas Turbine division for a year, and for the next three years he watched it come true as he continued to direct AGT's burgeoning jet engine activities. It was a period during which the division expanded geographically, sharply increased employment, established basic management and organizational concepts still in use today, began development of an engine that would become perhaps the world's best known high performance powerplant, defined the important relationship of the engine/airframe combination in total aircraft system design, and moved boldly into small aircraft engine development.

When, in 1955, Jim LaPierre was named executive vice president of the General Electric Company, he became the first of a number of "graduates" of the aircraft engine business to move into corporate management.

His successor at AGT would be the second executive from GE's young aircraft engine organization to become a driving force in General Electric's corporate structure. Jack S. Parker, who retired at the end of 1979 as vice chairman and member of the board of directors of General Electric, was responsible for the company's entry into small engines as head of GE's aircraft engine business during the second half of the decade of the 1950s. It was a time when the expansion of the company's jet engine activities would include not only a move into civil aviation but also the development of the largest array of new engines—the majority of which are still in production—in GE's history.

1.

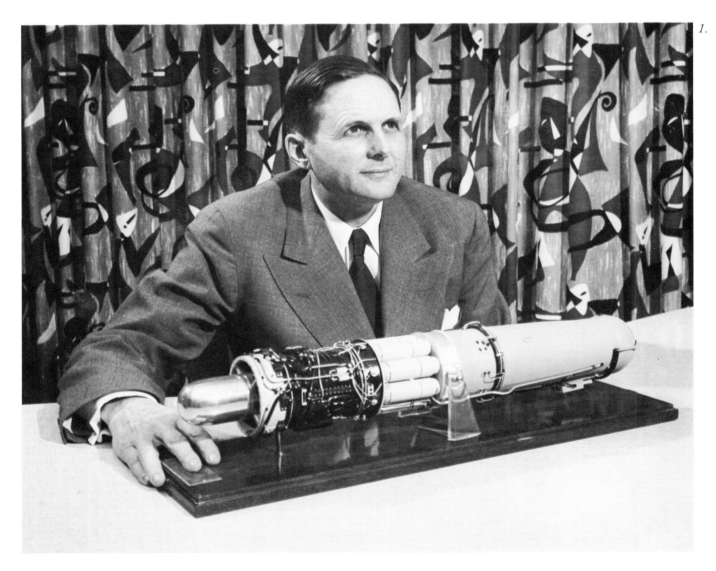

J47 production: up...down...and up again

Following its formal opening in 1949, the Lockland plant was the site of a rapid buildup of J47 production. GE conceived what became known as the "Lockland Plan"—a philosophy of production under which the thousands of components used in a jet engine were produced by specialized manufacturers all over the nation and flowed to a large central assembly point (Lockland) for final production. At the time more than 260 manufacturers were part of the supply chain. The Lockland Plan was one of the pioneering examples of "big business/small business" cooperation for mutual benefits—and received nationwide press coverage. (Today, more than 5,500 businesses in 45 states and 11 countries around the world supply parts for GE engines.)

But the Lockland Plan, along with the increase in J47 production, was almost killed before it had a chance to come to life. Early 1950 was a time for one of the many, periodic government economy waves which meant, among other things, a cutback in defense spending. The U.S. Air Force notified the company it would be necessary to reduce J47 deliveries. Some consideration was given to closing the Lockland facility (only two years after it had opened), but a compromise solution was reached to keep the plant in use. The USAF wanted to retain the facility as a defense production base, but in order to do so a considerable sacrifice in efficiency was required: the subcontractor manufacturing would have to be diverted back to Lockland. The carefully constructed network of suppliers stretching from ocean to ocean began to be dismantled.

Then, six weeks after the "notices of cancellation" had started going out to hundreds of vendors, came the United Nations (and U.S.) intervention in Korea—and the whole process was reversed! J47 production had to increase once again.

1. *Cramer W. "Jim" LaPierre.*
2. *J47 production line at Lockland Plant.*

2.

THE FIFTIES

The Korean conflict—and the requirement for stepped-up deliveries to the USAF of GE-powered North American F-86s and Boeing B-47s—called for expansion of Lockland's manufacturing. Bert Mahoney, a GE manufacturing veteran from Schenectady, was named Lockland manufacturing manager in 1951. Recognizing the complexities of a product made up of thousands of parts produced by a nationwide supplier network—and one that was subject to continuing engineering changes resulting from technology advances—Mahoney developed a prudent philosophy: "Don't start anything until you can finish it. Don't start the assembly of an engine until you have all the parts!"

Key members of the Mahoney manufacturing team were Gene Firestone, who would become the division's general manager, and Ralph Medros, today the Aircraft Engine Group's product quality general manager.

J47 production continued in Lynn under the direction of Larry Callahan, to whom had been imparted the wisdom of Gus Berg, the manufacturing leader responsible for the River Works' earlier wartime production achievements. Callahan had served as Berg's assistant manager of manufacturing.

Two major manufacturing accomplishments of Callahan's Lynn team resulted in savings of millions of dollars in the cost of J47 production.

Facing a problem of compressor rotor instability in early J47 production models, the manufacturing engineers conceived the idea of assembling the engine vertically to assure total integrity and stability of the engine buildup. Vertical assembly also resulted in more efficient production. All J47s were ultimately built that way.

From the Lynn team also came the proposal for the "random one-in-ten testing" concept that eliminated the re-testing of every completed engine ready for acceptance off the assembly line. Instead of the costly procedure that called for each finished engine to be installed, hooked up and test run before shipment, the USAF inspectors would choose at random one engine in every ten for a test run. If any problem was indicated, the engines in that sequence would each have to be tested; if the test was positive, delivery was made. The USAF accepted the proposal and all J47 production switched to the procedure—at estimated savings to the government of several million dollars.

1.

J47 engine production reached a rate of 975 *per month* in 1953-54. (In the 1942-45 period a *grand total* of 271 I-As and I-16s had been produced.) Despite a nine-week Lockland plant strike in 1953, all J47s were delivered to North American and Boeing on schedule. Not a single aircraft shipment was delayed by the strike.

Because of the demand for J47s, two automotive manufacturers—Studebaker and Packard—were licensed to build the engine. Despite substantial assistance from General Electric manufacturing experts, both companies found it impossible to match GE's production costs, and production at their plants was stopped as soon as USAF requirements for the J47 declined.

The booming Lockland production unintentionally created another noise—in the local community. With a monthly delivery rate of some 500 engines, the new test cells created out of the old Wright facilities were being used night and day and the sounds emanating from their stacks created the first community relations problem. After an original warm welcome from the Greater Cincinnati populace—the move to Lockland of a major corporation had generated thousands of new jobs and an impact on the local economy—the local burghers now weren't too sure about their new neighbor. The Lockland switchboard was frequently lit up with complaint calls, particularly at night.

Several steps were taken to resolve the local crisis: immediately begin the design and installation of better soundproofing in the cells; schedule engine tests to avoid evening hours; completely eliminate night-time running; and supply a plainly marked GE truck equipped with electronic sound measuring gear to cruise the northern Cincinnati area around the plant during engine tests. As a final step, the local community leaders and the press were notified of what was happening. The concern and action had an immediate impact. The complaints dropped significantly and GE and the community were once again at peace.

2.

1. *J47 vertical assembly at Lynn.*
2. *Bert Mahoney with J47 (above) and J73 engines.*
3. *Larry Callahan.*
4. *Ralph Medros.*

3.

4.

The Lockland aircraft engine plant location originally had some unfortunate connotations for many Cincinnatians. Immediately following the end of World War II, the U.S. government-owned Wright facility—which at its peak had employed more than 35,000 people—was shut down. For a time the impact on the Cincinnati economy was monumental.

Community leaders feared the same when the Korean involvement ended. After all, the parallel was almost exact: a major corporation building aircraft engines in a government facility under wartime circumstances.

General Electric management, however, had an entirely different plan: to acquire the property from the government and expand it, thus providing completely company-owned plant and equipment—and a more efficient operation.

As J47 production increased during the Korean War, GE occupied more and more of the Lockland plant it was still leasing from the U.S. government. In 1950 the company had erected a new engineering and production center north of the old Wright complex with an investment of $25 million. Although the majority of the former Wright facility was still government-owned, the large central production buildings were owned by Electric Auto-Lite. GE bought this property as part of its plan to take over the entire 450-acre (93 acres under roof) Lockland complex.

The massive refurbishing and housecleaning of the Lockland plant was generally not an appealing assignment for GE workers. There was an exception, however. One building in the complex had been leased out for use as a bonded warehouse for distilled whiskey. Volunteers by the hundreds stepped forward to undertake the task of cleaning out that one.

GE's active acquisition and expansion—and an assuring message to the community—were heralded in an advertisement in local newspapers: "As permanent as Fountain Square!" Fountain Square has always been the graphic symbol of Cincinnati. It is interesting to note that during major urban improvements in Cincinnati in the 1970s, the city's fountain was moved to accommodate the new downtown "face" of the city. GE's plant has not moved.

J47 engine design had first been laid down in 1946. Production ended ten years later—after the delivery of more than 35,000 units by GE and its licensees, Packard and Studebaker. Many more J47 engines had been programmed for manufacture by the USAF, but reliability improvements incorporated in the design over its lifetime had markedly increased the engine's time-between-overhaul (TBO) rate, permitting J47s to continue in operational service much longer than originally projected. As a result of the J47's longer life expectancy, further production was cancelled in 1956, resulting in a saving to the government of $200 million, according to USAF estimates.

1.

J47 advances state of the art

The J47 engine was the most-produced aircraft gas turbine in history. And it was responsible for a host of technical advances important to turbine technology—and to General Electric's future.

The J47 was derived from the GE TG-180/J35, an engine the leading industry trade journal, *Aviation Week*, called "the most widely specified American jet power plant" in a 1947 design analysis article. The magazine's analysis of the TG-180/J35 said, "the engine evidences an exceptional degree of design refinement, displaying a notable minimizing of exterior piping and gadgetry...[it] constitutes a remarkably clean installation."

In 1949 the J47 was the first turbojet certified for commercial operation by the Civil Aeronautics Administration (CAA). Although the engine met all of the federal standards for civil use, its certification was really largely an exercise for CAA officials to learn about gas turbines since no American aircraft manufacturer was yet ready to gamble on the design and construction of a civil jet transport. Nevertheless, valuable lessons for the future were learned by the government, by GE and by airframe developers of larger, multi-engine aircraft, including Boeing, producer of the J47-powered B-47.

One of the technical challenges that became evident as jet-powered aircraft of the postwar period flew higher and faster was icing of the engines—both a dangerous condition and one severely detrimental to performance. In Lynn, engineer Joe Buechel, who had gained his first turbine experience on the J35, worked with Neil Burgess to develop an anti-icing system for the J47. The only data available were some basic studies on the general subject produced by the National Advisory Committee for Aeronautics (NACA). Burgess and Buechel developed a system of channeling heated compressed air from the engine into hollow compressor vanes—a technique still in use today. But the never-before-tried system had to be tested under realistic icing conditions. In-flight tests were obviously too dangerous.

To Nick Carter fell the dubious privilege of spending an extended period away from the hustle and bustle of the River Works—during the winter of 1948-49—atop the 6,288-foot peak of Mount Washington in New Hampshire's White Mountains. Carter and his team lived there for several months and saw temperatures reach 40 degrees below zero with winds up to 140 miles per hour—ideal for anti-icing engine tests if not for much else. The Burgess-Buechel-Carter refinement paid off. The J47 became the world's first anti-iced engine, setting the stage for safer, higher-flying civil and military airplanes.

1. *Lockland plant.*
2. *R.L. "Nick" Carter.*
3. *J.C. Buechel.*
4. *Mount Washington test site.*

The J47 was also the first U.S. turbojet to use an electronically-controlled afterburner, a device to augment engine power at takeoff and during altitude acceleration that had originally been studied in the Army Air Corps Power Plant Laboratory as early as 1943. The first job assigned Edward Woll when he joined GE in 1946 was to design an afterburner for the TG-180. Ed Woll (who would become Aircraft Engine Group engineering vice president and a powerful advocate of gas turbine technology progress) had worked with Colonel Don Keirn at Wright Field, among other things experimenting with afterburners for the GE I-16 engine. Woll, together with Ed Ledbetter, developed a variable afterburner for the TG-180 that was subsequently refined for the J47 to include electronic controls linked with engine controls. The same basic concept is used today in afterburning military engines.

1.

The afterburning J47 engine (J47-GE-17) was produced for the North American F-86D, an advanced model of the Sabrejet series. The original J47 had replaced an Allison-built J35 in the F-86. GE's Ed Specht worked closely with North American's John Young and other aircraft designers, demonstrating that the J47 had more power than the J35 in the same frame size. The afterburning J47 made it ideal for the new interceptor's mission. The F-86 was also responsible for bringing to GE a test pilot who would help the company establish new flight test standards for engine manufacturers—Roy Pryor.

After leaving the U.S. Air Force, Pryor applied to North American for a test pilot slot. Because GE was then having problems with the J47's electronic controls—causing delays in airplane deliveries—North American couldn't fully utilize those pilots already employed. But they knew GE was in the process of leasing an F-86D so they could better understand—and solve—their controls problems. "Why not try GE," suggested the North American people to the experienced F-86 pilot. Pryor, known throughout his career as a professional, engineering-oriented test pilot, helped the GE team solve the engine control problem—and get the engines and F-86s back on schedule. Flying the leased F-86D out of the newly-created GE Flight Test Center at Edwards Air Force Base, California, Pryor provided land-locked engineers with realistic "game" conditions.

2.

3.

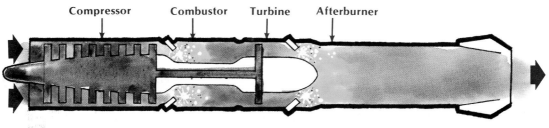

Compressor   Combustor   Turbine   Afterburner

Afterburning Turbojet Engine

1. *Edward Woll.*
2. *Afterburner J47 (above) and dry J47 engines.*
3. *Roy Pryor (left) and Virgil Weaver with J47-powered F-86D at Edwards AFB.*

THE FIFTIES

GE's Flight Test Center—closely tied to the USAF flight test efforts and the Southern California aviation industry because of its location at the Edwards base—became a focal point in the '50s (and the '60s and '70s as well) not only for "proving" GE engines under actual flight conditions but also for the evolution of the concept of integrating engine and airframe design. That close liaison of airframe and engine designers was to prove a significant factor in GE's aviation progress in the years ahead.

GE's Flight Test Center "proved" not only engines—but engineers as well. Richard B. Smith, who had started at Lynn, earned his early stripes at Edwards helping to solve the engine control problem on the J47-powered F-86D. Dick Smith would later become a strong influence in GE's commercial engine business. From 1952 through 1973 GE's flight operation was headed by Virgil Weaver, a pillar of the desert flight test community.

1. *GE Flight Test Center, Edwards Air Force Base, in the 1950s.*

2. *Richard B. Smith, Fred Preston, Colonel William Barnes, Cliff Massey and Charles Schumate at Edwards AFB.*

1.

2.

THE FIFTIES

Sequence of engines planned

In the late 1940s and early 1950s, with the J47 well into development and production, Aircraft Gas Turbine division management ordered a study of future military and civil aircraft planning—and the powerplants required. Four completely different approaches evolved from this study.

In 1947 the Air Force had funded Pratt & Whitney for an engine study that eventually resulted in the J57 turbojet. At the same time the USAF planners and Power Plant Lab also began to look for a very high thrust engine. From this interest came GE's XJ53, a 1948-originated design calling for a thrust output of nearly 17,000 pounds —double the thrust of most engines in existence at that time.

Projected weight of the engine was 6,000 pounds—3,500 pounds more than the J47. Both the thrust and engine weight made it by far the most powerful and largest jet engine of its time. It was, of course, an axial flow design.

When the first design was completed and projected weight indicated a total of more than 8,300 pounds, the engineers knew they had a problem. By the time the first engine ran on test in March, 1951, a combination of Lynn and Schenectady engineering experts had succeeded in reducing the weight to 7,950 pounds with the engine delivering the unprecedented power of 17,950 pounds of thrust. However, it was painfully apparent to both GE and the USAF that the engine was entirely too large—no airframe then contemplated called for an engine of that size—and that further efforts to reduce weight would result in unsatisfactory performance characteristics. The XJ53 engine development was discontinued in September, 1953.

But GE engineers had gained hard-won experience in the design of large, high thrust engines from the XJ53. A number of problems were solved, including efficient utilization of large, complex parts and the design of engine controls for a powerplant with a high pressure ratio (the ratio of air pressure increase from front to back of the compressor). These lessons proved invaluable for later engines.

1. XJ53 turbojet engine.
2. Jim LaPierre (left) and Virgil Weaver with Turbodyne turboprop engine.

1.

A second turboprop for GE

From an unlikely source—an aircraft company—came a second approach to future engine development. In the early 1940s a Czech-born engineer, Vladimir Pavlecka, had come to Jack Northrop, president of Northrop Aircraft, with an idea for a gigantic gas turbine-driven propeller (turboprop) engine. The company had the engine in development both during and after World War II—intended primarily for use on Jack Northrop's early Flying Wing bomber design. Northrop had received outside engine design consultation from two respected names in propulsion: Dr. Theodore Von Karman of the California Institute of Technology and Frank Whittle. The USAF in the late 1940s contracted for the development of the YB-35 Flying Wing (designated the EB-35B as a flying test bed) to be powered by six J35s, with additional power on the final version of the airplane provided by two of the giant turboprops, by then called the Turbodyne. In addition, the Turbodyne was planned as power for the new USAF B-52 long range bomber. Two USAF decisions brought General Electric into the Turbodyne picture.

When the Air Force changed the powerplant design of the B-52 from turboprop to turbojet, work was discontinued on the EB-35B. And, when the Air Force decided in early 1950 to consolidate its many and varied engine development programs, the Secretary of the Air Force requested that GE take over Turbodyne development. The company was back in the turboprop business—but, as it happened, only briefly.

Although the engine delivered 11,500 horsepower (it was the most powerful turboprop in the world at that time), studies by both engineers and management of the Aircraft Gas Turbine division concluded that the requirements for such a large turboprop engine—either military or civil—were extremely limited. Jim LaPierre made the decision in 1951 to discontinue further development of the engine.

2.

THE FIFTIES

A growth J47

The third approach to the continued evolution of jet engine development was a logical step: "grow" the J47. Started in mid-1949, the growth engine originally was called the J47-21 (and soon redesignated the J73). It was conceived as a 50 percent growth step beyond the original J47. The engine derived many of its design features from the XJ53. In fact, Neil Burgess, who headed the J73 program, later recalled that the J73 and XJ53 were "sister and brother." The J73 featured GE's first two-stage turbine, the highest compressor pressure ratio up to the time, the first variable inlet guide vanes, the first cannular (combustion chambers with circumferential inner and outer combustion shells) combustor, and the first use of titanium.

The J73 engine went on test in mid-1950, a year after start of design. An afterburning version was tested in late 1951. At that time the project was headed by Hilliard W. Paige.

During the late 1940s and early 1950s, the U.S. military had four separate development engines in the same thrust class: Pratt & Whitney J57, Westinghouse J40, Allison J71, and GE J73. The J73 was in the 9,000 pound thrust class—somewhat less power than the other three—and represented a conservative approach.

One potential application for the new J73 was a four engined version of the Boeing B-47 as an alternative to the six J47 engines on the original design. The four-jet B-47 proposal was studied with J73s, J57s, and J71s. None of these engines made a significant aircraft performance improvement over six J47s and the Boeing airplane continued its production and operational life as originally conceived.

1.

2.

82

North American's F-86s had been performing well in the skies over Korea and the U.S. Air Force and North American believed even more improvements could be achieved in the successful design. The airframe designers developed the F-86H, incorporating aerodynamic features such as large wing flaps and other improvements that gave the airplane a shorter turning radius and, with a more powerful engine, higher combat speeds. The J73 growth version of the J47 powering original F-86 models provided the additional thrust. GE engineers incorporated a "tail pipe augmentation" (TPA) system in the J73 as the answer to the requirement for a "war emergency rating" for the engine. The system consisted of a unique combustor, with extra fuel injection, added to the engine's tailpipe. TPA boosted the J73's takeoff power by 10 percent and altitude performance by 20 percent.

Despite the added power of the J73 and the aerodynamic improvements made on the F-86H, the advent of an entire new generation of so-called "Century Series" fighters (F-100, F-101, F-102, F-104, F-105, F-106) for the U.S. Air Force shortly made the airframe/engine combination obsolete. J73 engine production was terminated in January, 1956. A total of 870 engines had been built—all for the F-86H Sabrejet.

In addition to the important technical "firsts" achieved on the J73 engine, several young engineers who would make lasting contributions to GE's aircraft engine business received their baptism under fire during the five years of the engine's life: James N. Krebs, later to become the group's military engine vice president; Perry Egbert, a major figure in the early stages of GE's J79; Jerry Pederson, George Hardgrove and John Melzer, all of whom would make substantial technical contributions to the wide spectrum of GE gas turbines of the '50s, '60s and '70s.

3.

THE FIFTIES

The engine of the future

In 1952 Aircraft Gas Turbine division general manager Jim LaPierre said: "The division will aim always toward leadership in meeting the performance requirements established by the aircraft makers, the military agencies, the airlines, and the others who together create the tools of aviation...our sincere intention [is] to carry on the leadership inherited from our General Electric steam and gas turbine predecessors."

The Moss gas turbine concept had been ready for the requirements of the turbosupercharger in the early years; the Moss/Warren/Streid/Warner aircraft gas turbine studies had anticipated the needs that led to the P-59 flight in the '40s; the Burgess-led team had developed a J47 that met the needs of the 1950s. LaPierre saw to it that General Electric would lead in anticipating the requirements of the '60s and '70s.

From this basic management attitude came the fourth—and most successful—approach to an engine for the future. The design, begun in 1951, was built around a unique concept for achieving high performance, low weight and reliable operation. It would evolve into the company's most famous and longest production span engine—the J79.

1. Variable stator mechanism.
2. Dr. Chap Walker (left) and Gerhard Neumann with GOL-1590 engine.

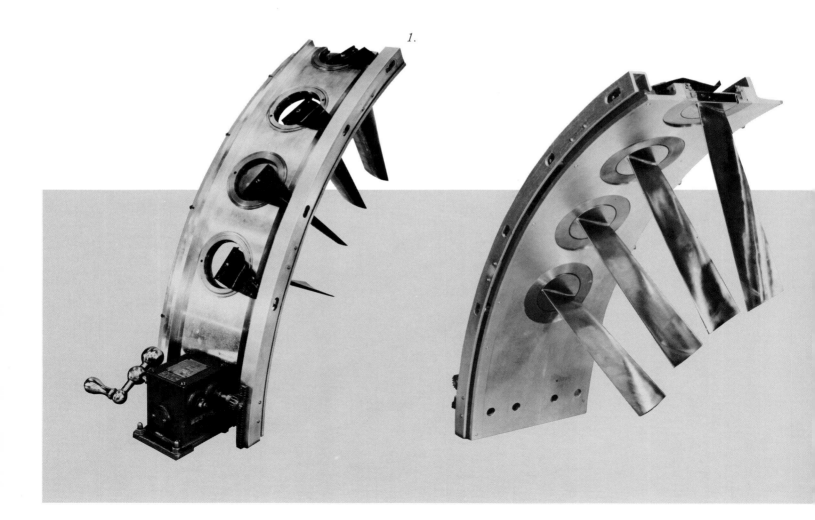

1.

The young German engineer who had made his first mark on General Electric's aircraft engine business when he fixed the mechanical problems of the mammoth Lynn compressor test facility was a five-year GE veteran in 1953. Gerhard Neumann credits Sam Puffer with "taking me under his wing...and starting my career at GE." During his first five years with the company he had not only been successful in making the compressor test chamber workable, but had been placed in charge of engine development testing at Lynn. There, Neumann had developed a mechanical device to achieve much-sought-after higher compressor pressures. Neumann was promoted to head Lynn's preliminary design operation and his group developed what was called the Variable Stator Experimental Engine (VSXE—or, as this small band of engineering pioneers called it, the "very sexy" engine). The VSXE used a mechanical linkage to change the angle of the stator blades (blades affixed in rows to the compressor's casing which alternate with the compressor blades affixed to the rotating central shaft). The device increased compressor air pressure and helped eliminate compressor stall.

The team built a hardware model of the variable stator mechanism from XJ53 parts and, despite the pessimism of some veteran GE engine designers who believed the mechanically variable blades would vibrate, leak air and degrade the compressor's efficiency, the 10-engineer group pressed their case.

Word of the unorthodox design reached Jim LaPierre and, without announcing a reason for the meeting, he invited Neumann to lunch. Over Boston scrod, the division general manager received a briefing on the VSXE from an enthusiastic but very surprised Neumann. When LaPierre asked how much it would cost to build a test compressor, Neumann—completely unprepared for such an eventuality—guessed "half a million dollars." LaPierre said "You have it."

2.

The test compressor was constructed and run. It produced an efficiency so high the engineers thought their instrumentation must be in error. They rechecked the test equipment. It was OK. The test results must be correct. The design was a resounding success.

Gerhard Neumann's association with the new variable stator—and with the eventual development of the J79 engine—was temporarily interrupted when he was transferred to the Lockland plant location of the newly created Aircraft Nuclear Propulsion department, a secret effort under the direction of Roy Shoults (the GE engineer who had first gathered information on the Whittle engine in England in 1941). At ANPD, Neumann helped modify a J47 engine that was the core of the world's first turbine engine to run on nuclear energy. He also helped design an advanced engine with a variable stator compressor for ANPD.

Neumann was soon back in the aircraft engine division. (ANPD, because of its unique energy source and top secret status, was under contract to the Atomic Energy Commission as well as the U.S. Air Force and was not an organizational part of the aircraft engine division.) LaPierre, aware of the wide difference of opinion within his own organization regarding the basic design principle for the next generation of high performance aircraft engines, established two competing engine design teams. Variable stators were one way of achieving the high pressure ratios and stall avoidance necessary for high performance engines. Another was the dual rotor, in which two different shafts operated the forward and aft sections of the compressor separately. The Pratt & Whitney J57 engine had a dual rotor. The two teams would explore these concepts. Gerhard Neumann and Dr. Chapman Walker headed the variable stator team.

After nearly a year of concentrated effort, including periodic Saturday review meetings with LaPierre to ensure that common ground rules were being observed, the fateful decision was to be made at an ''offshore'' conference where each of the competitors would be given equal time to present their designs and arguments.

In October, 1952, at French Lick (a well-known spa in the rolling Indiana countryside), the far-reaching GE decision was made: proceed with the development of the variable stator engine. Having made the decision, LaPierre gave Neumann the go-ahead to establish a program and build a demonstrator. The GOL-1590, predecessor to the J79, was begun in 1953.

1.

1. *GOL-1590 demonstrator engine.*
2. *GOL-1590 project engineering team.*

The team is assembled

Already fully confident of the design of the variable stator compressor, Neumann's first task was to assemble the team that would build and test the complete demonstrator engine. He chose Bert Sells, Joe O'Toole, Jim Krebs, Bob Holland, Bob Ingraham, Dick Bradshaw, Bill Collier, Wes Hurley and, to furnish objective external technical counsel, a former dean of the University of California's school of engineering, Mike O'Brien. O'Brien continued to provide GE's aircraft engine management with sage analytical judgment through the 1970s.

Objectives laid down for the new engine were relatively simple in concept, but challenging in execution: (1) efficient performance both at cruise speeds of Mach 0.9 (nine-tenths the speed of sound) and at combat speeds of Mach 2 (twice the speed of sound); (2) provide increased thrust for these greater speeds while reducing fuel consumption and engine weight.

The GOL-1590 was a single rotor, variable stator compressor, high pressure ratio, lightweight turbojet engine. It would be a test vehicle to demonstrate these concepts in one engine package. Thrust rating was 13,200 pounds with a total engine weight, including afterburner, of 2,935 pounds.

2.

After nearly a year of frenzied effort the first engine was ready to go to test at 5 a.m. on December 16, 1953. Although most of the team had worked all night, the atmosphere in the test cell was electric with excitement. A mutual commitment had been made to run the engine up to full speed on the first run. As the test cell technician slowly pushed the throttle forward and the engine began to roar, building up to its full power, most eyes were on the instrumentation that displayed the various test points being achieved. The few who could crowd around were intently peering through the small, insulated window that provided a limited view of the engine running inside the giant test cell. Suddenly an ear-splitting explosion shook the cell, the adjacent instrumentation room and its occupants.

The forward section of the engine slumped to the floor, compressor blades sliced through their casing and the engine screeched to a stop. As soon as it was safe, the cell doors were opened and the shocked team began to inspect the debris. The answer to what had happened came quickly. The front connecting link that anchored the engine in the permanent test cell structure—commonly called the "dog bone"—had been improperly fabricated. It ruptured under stress as the engine revved up to full power. The engine was not at fault—but there certainly was a problem with supposedly insignificant test cell parts.

Many members of the GOL-1590 team drove home that morning bone tired and nauseated. But, it was back to the benches and by February, 1954, the rebuilt engine had logged nearly six hours of running time. The variable stator mechanism had been proven. Performance was as predicted. An entirely new generation of turbojet engines had been demonstrated.

1.

Mach 2 in view

While the GOL-1590 demonstrator progressed, GE's management and technical team was working closely with the Air Force, including the Power Plant Laboratory's Cliff Simpson, on study contracts for supersonic engines. From these studies evolved the X24A, an engine with 9,290 pounds of thrust (without afterburner) capable of providing supersonic speed in the right airplane. With the design studies in hand, GE engineers were confident they could produce the world's first Mach 2 engine. This confidence generated an expression, ''Mach 2 In View,'' that was promptly designed into posters placed prominently throughout GE's engineering operations. A few were unobtrusively placed in Air Force offices.

In late 1952 the X24A was selected by the USAF for further development and designated the MX2118. General Electric had entered the high performance, lightweight engine field. GE used the GOL-1590 as a demonstrator to support the new engine.

The MX2118 Project was established in December, 1952, with Perry Egbert in charge.

GE's Ed Woll and Jim Bingham had been working with Convair Ft. Worth's Bob Widmer in support of a series of studies being conducted by Convair on the next generation bomber for the USAF. One of the studies had resulted in an Air Force contract for the MX1964 (later to become the B-58). Although the bomber had originally been designed for the J57, the new GE engine weighed 2,000 pounds less than the competitive engine and gave the Convair airplane a marked improvement in performance.

The Air Force and Convair selected the MX2118 (ultimately designated the J79) for the B-58 and an entirely new era in engine/airframe design compatibility was under way.

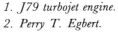
1. J79 turbojet engine.
2. Perry T. Egbert.

2.

Until the creation of the J79, most engines had been designed essentially independently of the aircraft they eventually powered. Engine developers such as General Electric traditionally tried to anticipate the broad requirements of the aircraft designers, but the development of specific powerplants and airframes usually progressed independently. The high performance requirements of the new Mach 2 engine and its critical marriage with equally high performance airplanes such as the B-58 demanded that the powerplant and airframe evolve as a single system.

The J79 was the first GE engine designed with the sophistication provided by already developed and demonstrated components and advanced instrumentation techniques for projecting test performance, along with extensive knowledge of how to utilize newly developed materials. The division's Advanced Design group formed in 1950 under the direction of Gene Stoeckly had helped to make possible the high performance J79.

Although Perry Egbert had been responsible for specifying the original designs released for manufacturing, he retired in ill health before the first engine went to test. In October, 1953, Neil Burgess was named to head the project. The first J79 was run in a Lockland test cell in June, 1954.

1. *Convair B-58 and J79.*
2. *Marty Hemsworth, Neil Burgess, and Perry Egbert.*
3. *J79 installed in B-45 flying test bed.*
4. *First J79 on way to test cell, June, 1954.*

1.

J79 flight tests begin—and produce an industry first

2.

3.

The J79 engine was first airborne in an unlikely location: Schenectady, New York. A legacy from the days when General Electric's aviation activities were divided between Lynn and Schenectady, the company's General Engineering Laboratory continued to operate a Flight Test division at the Schenectady, New York airport. Slung in the bomb bay of a specially instrumented J47-powered North American B-45 Tornado, the J79 went into the air for the first time on May 20, 1955. In flight, the engine was tested by lowering it from the bomb bay into the air stream. The four J47s were shut down and for a brief period, the lone J79 propelled the B-45 through the skies above upper New York State. The tests were successful and the designers moved confidently into the next stage of flight test. It would result in an industry first.

The B-45 "test bed" flights bolstered the confidence of the J79 project team as they approached their real flight test goal: to provide the airframe designers with a flight proven powerplant that had already been wrung out by the engine maker before it was installed in the ultimate production airplane. No other engine developer had ever before done this.

4.

In late 1953, GE had leased a Douglas XF4D from the Navy (the airplane was the first "X"—or test—model of this airplane built by Douglas) to fly a J79-powered airplane for the first time. GE's Flight Test Center manager Virgil Weaver, chief test pilot Roy Pryor, engineer Dick Smith and their team of technicians pulled the original single Westinghouse J40 and began aircraft modification to marry the more powerful engine to the airframe. The airplane's inlet ducting had to be changed significantly to accommodate the J79's increased airflow. The entire airframe modification, including complex ducting from the twin air inlets on each side of the XF4D fuselage, was done by the GE technicians. This was truly a pioneering move to make major modifications on an existing airframe to accommodate the initial flight of the world's first Mach 2 powerplant.

In mid-1955 the technicians began to install the J79. By late November, Pryor and Smith were ready for ground testing—engine runup to full power with the airplane anchored to the air strip apron. Each step was taken carefully, cautiously.

More than a week of trying, fixing, re-trying and refining finally culminated in the first taxi tests on the five mile-plus Edwards Air Force Base runway. After the ground tests, Pryor and Smith called for additional fine tuning. On December 8, 1955, they believed all was in readiness.

The engine had been fully instrumented to transmit all of the test parameters of engine operation to the Air Force telemetering stations atop the low mountains surrounding the Muroc desert. In fact, the test instrumentation had constituted a major challenge in the airframe modifications: how to fit all of the wiring trunks and leads from the engine into already compact spaces within the existing aircraft design.

1. *XF4D powered by J79 on first flight.*
2. *"Tiger By The Tail" jacket patch worn by J79 jet pilots.*

1.

In his high-visibility-orange flight test suit, Pryor was a striking figure as he climbed in and out of the XF4D on that day assuring himself that the J79 was ready to power an airplane on its own.

The winter sun was sinking quickly toward the California mountains when, after a final high speed taxi run, Pryor steered the little "hot rod" airplane toward the end of Edwards runway 4, turned, and held the brakes while the J79 climbed toward takeoff power. At 4:23 p.m., GE's chief test pilot released the brakes. The XF4D began to roll...rotated...the wheels were off the concrete...the world's most advanced engine had lifted the airplane into the desert sky. A loud cheer went up from the small band of earth-bound stalwarts—J79 project management, Flight Test Center engineers and technicians, and still and motion picture crews gathered for the historic event. The moment had been several years in coming and every pair of eyes was riveted upward in an effort to follow the small silver airplane as it climbed into the rapidly darkening sky.

By the time Pryor brought the XF4D back onto the safety of the Edwards runway, after a nearly 40 minute flight, it was dark. Spotlights illuminated the little circle on the desert base where the small crowd awaited the results, listening to radio communications and checking the telemetering tests relayed to them. In classic first flight tradition, Pryor taxied up, opened the cockpit canopy and, with a broad grin, raised a gloved thumb into the air. The flight was a success.

"The airplane had fantastic acceleration and performance compared to anything I have ever flown before," the test pilot reported as he greeted well-wishers gathered around the airplane. "It felt like I had a tiger by the tail!" was Pryor's summary—and that soon became the hallmark of the J79 program: "Tiger By The Tail!"

In the months that followed, the XF4D was used to wring out many of the early J79 development kinks, including afterburner and engine controls. GE would deliver a flight proven engine to the airframe designers—an industry first.

2.

THE FIFTIES

J79 applications broadened

The Mach 2 J79 had originally been matched with the Convair B-58 Hustler by the U.S. Air Force during the rapid development progress of the revolutionary powerplant in the early 1950s. But it soon became evident that mating the engine with other high performance airplanes then in planning stages could mean an entirely new generation of defense airpower.

Lockheed's Kelly Johnson had designed an equally revolutionary airframe in his Burbank, California "Skunk Works": the F-104 Starfighter. The F-104 became known as the "missile with a man in it" because of its stiletto-like fuselage and short, thin wings. The airplane had originally been designed around the Curtiss Wright J65 (which was derived from the British Bristol Sapphire) and the first J65-powered flight tests indicated that with that engine the F-104 was just slightly faster than the speed of sound (Mach 1).

Lockheed and GE designers began airframe/engine studies using the J79. It was soon apparent that with the new engine the Starfighter would be a Mach 2 (twice the speed of sound) airplane. Following the GE XF4D flight testing, an F-104 had been modified and the single J79 was installed. Both Lockheed and GE began flight tests. (Roy Pryor called the F-104 "the greatest airplane I ever flew...although not for 'stick and rudder' pilots...it must be flown with a professional attitude.") Actually, the Starfighter was the first aircraft after the XF4D to be powered by the J79 since the B-58 flew nine months after the F-104.

1.

The F-104 went into service with the USAF Air Defense Command and became the world's fastest interceptor, setting a series of world speed, altitude and time-to-climb records.

But, interestingly, the F-104's greatest fame came from its use abroad. A consortium of European nations—Germany, Belgium, Italy, and the Netherlands—and Japan selected the Starfighter as their principal air defense system for the late 1950s and 1960s. The U.S. government, in partnership with Lockheed and General Electric, established a far-flung licensing and manufacturing network in these five countries. The F-104 program has been credited with regenerating the utterly destroyed aviation industries of a number of nations. Most German, Belgian, Italian, Dutch and Japanese aerospace industry giants of the 1970s continued their recovery from World War II by building under license F-104 airframes, J79 engines and all of the thousands of support systems that went into this highly advanced aircraft.

1. Herman "Fish" Salmon with Lockheed F-104 Starfighter, the "missile with a man in it."

2. J79-powered F-104s in service with West Germany, Spain, Netherlands, Japan, Italy and Belgium.

2.

The complex production network for the Starfighter required extensive technical assistance from U.S. experts as American drawings were translated into the metric system and the knowledge of advanced U.S. design and manufacturing technology was transferred to the consortium. Although General Electric had long been recognized as an international company, its international presence was considerably magnified during the Starfighter program. In setting up the J79's worldwide licensing and production network, Ray Small earned much of the credit for this expanded influence. Others who were responsible for the licensing program included Gene Firestone, Bob Garvin, Tom Harmon, Joe LaMarca and Charley Steele.

This program, together with the earlier T58 licensing program with deHavilland of England, gave the relatively young Aircraft Gas Turbine division organization its initial exposure to worldwide business...providing liaison, advice and counsel and frequent "hands on" assistance to the government establishment and manufacturers within the Starfighter consortium.

In 1959, in recognition of the F-104's achievements, GE's Gerhard Neumann and Neil Burgess, Lockheed's Kelly Johnson, USAF Lt. Col. Howard C. Johnson (who set a world land-plane altitude record of 91,249 feet in the F-104) and Major Walter W. Irwin (who set the world straightaway speed record of 1,404.09 miles per hour in the aircraft) were jointly named winners of aviation's most prestigious award, the Collier Trophy, for 1958. The J79-powered F-104 later became the first manned aircraft to exceed 100,000 feet when it set a 103,395 feet altitude mark—nearly 20 miles high.

1.

2.

The J79 in navy blue

The J79 had started life as a U.S. Air Force program, but the mating of the engine with a U.S. Navy airplane provided GE with the powerplant's greatest and longest production.

The Navy and Grumman had selected the J79 to power an advanced version of their F11F fighter, the F11F-1F. Two flight test demonstrators were built and Grumman offered the airplane to the Air Force but that service's selection of the F-104 ruled out another airplane. The F11F-1F competed with the F-104 in the international marketplace as well. GE was in the unique position of providing the powerplant for both of the leading competitors for this multi-million-dollar business. The F11F-1F program was terminated when the European consortium and the Japanese selected the F-104.

But the Navy had been exposed to the J79, and GE designers and Bill Graves in the St. Louis office began to work with McDonnell Aircraft in St. Louis to match the new supersonic powerplant with the F4H Phantom II, latest in a long line of McDonnell high performance airplanes for the Navy's air arm. Two J79s installed in the new Phantom gave that airplane Mach 2 capability and, together with the F4H's aerodynamic design, made that airframe/engine combination (later designated the F-4) the "hottest" military weapon system in the sky.

1. *Ramond E. Small.*

2. *Collier Trophy: Walt Irwin, Howard Johnson, Vice President Richard M. Nixon, Gerhard Neumann, Neil Burgess, Kelly Johnson.*

3. *J79-powered Grumman F11F-1F, and*

4. *McDonnell F-4 Phantom II.*

3.

4.

THE FIFTIES

The U.S. Navy selected the J79-powered F-4 as its primary fleet air defense airplane; the U.S. Marine Corps adopted it for both air combat and ground attack missions; the Air Force chose the F-4 for both tactical and air defense roles (a significant achievement considering that one normally prideful military service rarely selects an airplane developed by another); and the Phantom was eventually selected by eight other nations as their principal air defense aircraft.

By mid-1979 McDonnell (now McDonnell Douglas) had built and delivered more than 5,000 F-4s.

In addition to the F-4 and F11F-1F, the Navy also selected the J79 to power the North American A3J (later RA-5) Vigilante attack and reconnaissance aircraft that for most of the 1960s and 1970s provided the principal ''eyes'' for the U.S. fleet in its reconnaissance role. Moreover, the J79 powered the Chance Vought Regulus II. The Regulus has been called the U.S.' first ''cruise missile.''

By the end of the 1970s, nearly 17,000 General Electric J79s had been produced. The engine continues in production for the McDonnell Douglas F-4 Phantom. That makes a 30-year life span for the world's first Mach 2 engine and, at the time of its conception, the most advanced turbojet powerplant ever designed.

J79-powered:
1. *Chance Vought Regulus II;*
2. *North American A3J Vigilante;*
3. *5,000th McDonnell Douglas F-4 Phantom II.*

Engine business and organization both expand

J47 production in 1953 was in full swing; the Lockland plant had grown to accommodate the company's burgeoning business; development of the J79 was proceeding under contract to the USAF; and it was clear that the Aircraft Gas Turbine division's organization and future product planning had to be reviewed and a finite path established if the business was to continue to grow.

Jim LaPierre selected Jack Parker, who had joined General Electric in 1950 after a management career in West Coast shipbuilding, to head a study committee charged with taking an energetic overview of the business. The committee's recommendations were to have far-reaching impact on the business for the next 27 years.

Briefly, the committee recommended that GE pursue *both* military and civil aircraft engine business. It established a path for the newly evolving J79 engine. And it urged that the company begin development of small aircraft gas turbines. (One such engine, the XT58 turboshaft, was already being studied at Lynn.)

In line with the committee's recommendations, LaPierre brought in a young woman executive who had first impressed him in 1947 when they were both working at the company's General Engineering Laboratory in Schenectady. Marion Kellogg, today a GE corporate vice president for consulting services and the company's top female executive, was chosen to head an organization study of the division.

1.

1. T58 project team: Les Asher, Larry Callahan, John Turner, Jack Parker, Ed Woll and Harold Hokanson.
2. Marion Kellogg.
3. Donald R. Lester.

The careers of LaPierre, Neumann and Kellogg had been remarkably intertwined. Right after LaPierre was named general manager of the division in late 1949, he brought Marion Kellogg to Lynn to help recruit much-needed engineers and in 1951 she was transferred to Lockland in charge of personnel. The staff she selected included men who have gone on to become key personnel relations executives both within and outside of General Electric. One of her staff hired during this time was Donald R. Lester, who would become the Aircraft Engine Group's manager of organization and manpower.

During her Lynn stint, Kellogg was inadvertently responsible for helping to advance the career of Gerhard Neumann. One of the engineers assigned to Neumann when he ran the Lynn engine development testing operation was Fred Brown, who was then on the company-wide engineering "Test Program." Under the test program—a traditional company training experience dating back more than 40 years—young engineering graduates were moved to different assignments within the company every few months in order to gain the broadest possible knowledge of GE techniques and practices. When the time came for Brown to move on to his next assignment, the paperwork for the trainee's transfer was sent to Neumann. The resolute German engineer balked. They were right in the middle of an important test procedure and Neumann said, "He can't go!" Marion Kellogg said, "He must go!" The impasse reached Jim LaPierre. Neumann pleaded his case—and Brown stayed. Before that, LaPierre had never heard of Gerhard Neumann. It was the first—but certainly not the last—time LaPierre was to hear of Neumann.

2.

3.

101

THE FIFTIES

On the basis of recommendations in the Kellogg studies of mid-1953, a new functional organization was established on October 1 of that year to make sure that no phase of the aircraft turbine business was ever neglected. In a May, 1954, article about GE's jet engines, *Business Week* magazine said, "AGT [the division] divided the job of jet development and production into steps and let each step become an autonomous unit."

The new organization established a Development department under David Cochran to come up with basic engineering principles for components that would give better performance and greater power (the GOL-1590 J79 demonstrator was developed here).

The responsibility for designing and producing prototypes of new engines was assigned to the Jet Engine department under George Fouch (J79 engineering and flight test were located here).

The quantity production of engines was the responsibility of the Evendale Operating department under Bert Mahoney (by then the Lockland plant had become a part of the newly incorporated village of Evendale, Ohio, and the suburban Cincinnati GE facility has since been known colloquially as "Evendale").

At Lynn were the two additional departments of the newly created organization: the Aircraft Accessory Turbine department under Walter O'Connell, formed to develop a promising business in air turbine drives for aircraft electrical and hydraulic systems; and the Small Aircraft Engine department under Jack Parker, created to carry out the recommendations of the Parker-chaired committee and establish an entirely new facet of GE's jet engine business.

The 1954 *Business Week* article said the new organization "does what GE's top management demands—it pinpoints responsibility."

1.

1. David Cochran.
2. Jack Parker with T58 mockup.
3. Bill Meckley.
4. Bill Lawson.
5. T58-powered Sikorsky HSS-1 "Turbocopter"; and
6. Sikorsky HSS-2 type helicopters fly for four military services.

2.

Small engines start slowly

On January 1, 1953, following a study by a Lynn-based team composed of John Turner, Bill Lawson, Len Heurlin, Floyd Heglund and Bill Meckley, GE had made a proposal to the U.S. Navy for an 800 horsepower turboshaft engine weighing only 400 pounds to power helicopters. Called a "baby gas turbine," the XT58 won a Navy contract for something less than $3 million in June, 1953. That was the grand total of the business Jack Parker and his newly-appointed manager of engineering, Ed Woll, inherited when the Small Aircraft Engine department was formed in October, 1953.

LaPierre and Parker called for lengthy analyses of the XT58 design and its potential. The studies determined that the engine as submitted to the Navy not only provided less power than a team of veteran GE engineers believed was required, but it weighed too much. The small engine management team faced the task of telling its customer what type of engine the Navy *really* needed to power its new helicopters and getting the funds to change a design already under contract.

Following a lengthy Washington meeting with the Navy's Bureau of Aeronautics, and after a waiting period of several weeks, the Navy did change the contract and provided an additional $10 million for further XT58 development.

The first T58 produced 1,050 horsepower and weighed only 250 pounds. It was successfully tested in December, 1955, with a new compressor designed after a test failure of the uprated engine earlier in the year. Two T58s were installed in a Sikorsky HSS-1 (S-58)—replacing one piston engine—and the first flight of this "turbocopter" took place in February, 1957. Sikorsky management, anticipating the improved performance potential of a gas turbine-powered helicopter, petitioned the Navy for a contract to design an entirely new airframe around the T58. The result was the HSS-2 (the S-61 in commercial operations).

3.

4.

6.

5.

THE FIFTIES

In the late 1950s, Sikorsky and Kaman Aircraft, both headquartered in Connecticut, competed for a USN utility helicopter award. Both of the competitors' proposals called for GE T58 power. The Kaman SH-2 was selected. GE had its second small engine application, and the third was soon to follow.

Sikorsky pursued development of its unsuccessful entry into the Navy competition and the company's single-T58-powered S-62 became a very successful helicopter for the U.S. Coast Guard as well as for many passenger and cargo operators worldwide.

T58 applications grew steadily. The "baby gas turbine" was selected by Piasecki Helicopter (later Vertol, then Boeing Vertol) for the U.S. Army's UH-21D. The UH-21D flew in 1957, only a few months after the initial T58 flight in the Sikorsky HSS-1. The T58 became a quad-service engine when the U.S. Marine Corps ordered 600 Vertol HRB-1s. The HRB-1 later saw service with the U.S. Army and the Royal Canadian Air Force and entered commercial operation with New York Airways.

The major helicopter designers and producers—Sikorsky and Vertol—together with GE's small engine management had early seen the commercial potential of these true VTOL (vertical takeoff and landing) vehicles for a wide range of uses in places where conventional aircraft could not operate. In marketing to civil helicopter operators, GE earned its first exposure to commercial customers. The marketing lessons learned would be valuable later when commercial airline customers were being asked to consider GE engines.

CT58 commercial service with New York, Los Angeles and San Francisco Airways contributed substantially to the engine's improved reliability and increased performance in military and civil service.

Under the management of Jack Parker (and Gerhard Neumann after 1958), GE's small engine business at Lynn grew rapidly in the 1950s. Ray Letts, who played a significant role in Lynn's small engine manufacturing buildup, was later to become aircraft engine vice president of Group manufacturing. Output was raised from 25 to 35 engines per month with only modest investment in additional facilities and tooling.

1.

2.

3.

4.

During this period of Lynn small engine expansion the company opened two manufacturing facilities in Vermont—at Ludlow and Rutland. In the '60s, Hooksett, New Hampshire, became a third up-country plant, and towards the end of the decade, Albuquerque, New Mexico, was added as a southwest satellite. Despite its New England/upstate New York heritage, GE's aircraft engine management soon found that Vermonters were unique—even among New Englanders. When Vermont's governor visited one of the new plants, the townsfolk brought home-cooked, stick-to-the-ribs vittles to the local armory for a friendly reception. For an informative meeting with GE employees the locals offered the town movie theater. When it came to the subject of signing a contract for the local factory, the Vermonters didn't feel that was necessary: a "man's word" ought to be enough.

If the Vermonters were unusual, they shared the New England virtues of yankee ingenuity and thrift. At Rutland, the "pinch and roll" process was put in place to manufacture the small compressor blades—some no larger than a fingernail—needed for the "baby gas turbines." Over the years of small engine manufacturing, this relatively simple, high-production-rate technique, still in use today, saved the company millions of dollars.

J. Walter Herlihy, who headed both the Ludlow and Rutland plants, was most responsible for under-standing—and effectively utilizing—the unique nature of the Vermont operations. For years Walt Herlihy was known as "Mr. GE" in Vermont.

1. Ray Letts.
2. Ludlow, Vermont plant.
3. Rutland, Vermont plant.
4. Walt Herlihy.
5. LM100 marine engine.
6. SK-5 air cushion vehicle, powered by LM100.

T58 a foundation for GE small engines

The original T58 was an 800 horsepower engine. First test produced 1,050 horsepower. Increased turbine temperatures later in the 1950s raised its output to 1,250 horsepower. In the 1960s T58 output climbed to 1,500 horsepower and later to 1,800 horsepower—more than 70 percent growth over the first production models and all within the same frame size.

In 1959 a version of the T58, the LM100, was conceived for marine and industrial uses such as powering hydrofoil boats and air cushion vehicles and generating emergency standby electrical power.

The early challenges of the T58 and its later successes provided a spawning ground for a number of GE managers and engineers who would later play influential roles in the company's jet engine growth. In addition to Jack Parker, the T58 project was the early "stage" for Harold Hokanson, Van Claxton, Dave Gerry, Wally Bertaux, Fred Garry, Len Heurlin, Lynn Smith, Bill Crawford and Steve Chamberlin. Guy Shafer succeeded Jack Parker as project manager.

GE's first small gas turbine engine—starting from a single, small Navy contract—supplied the foundation for an entire generation of aircraft gas turbine products and people. Still in production as the decade of the '70s ended, the T58 is expected to continue as a GE engine product well into the 1980s.

5.

6.

The second small engine is born

Recognizing that their entire "product line" of small engines consisted of the T58, Parker and Woll shortly after the department was formed looked to the needs of the military in the later '50s and '60s. (Most gas turbine engines by then were being "grown" in thrust and size as fast as the designers could get them off the drawing boards; the philosophy underlying this new breed of aircraft powerplants was that "bigger, more powerful, was better.") Parker and Woll believed a really small turbojet engine of 2,500 pounds thrust in a small frame size would be required to power smaller, higher performance utility and support military airplanes.

The British were designing engines with a thrust-to-weight ratio of 6-to-1 (six pounds of thrust output for every pound of engine weight). Woll and his engineers believed they could design a 10-to-1 thrust/weight engine with about 2,500 pounds of thrust. That meant the engine would weigh only 250 pounds. GE actually proposed three engines to the USAF with a thrust-to-weight ratio of 10-to-1 with pressure ratios of 5-to-1, 7-to-1 and 12-to-1.

As it turned out, the Air Force was looking for a small turbojet for a new missile it was studying, the McDonnell GAM-72/Green Quail decoy to be used with the B-52 bomber. The "little" jet engine was the answer. A USAF contract for $3.5 million for the 7-to-1 proposal was awarded to GE. The J85 engine became GE's second small engine in late 1954.

1.

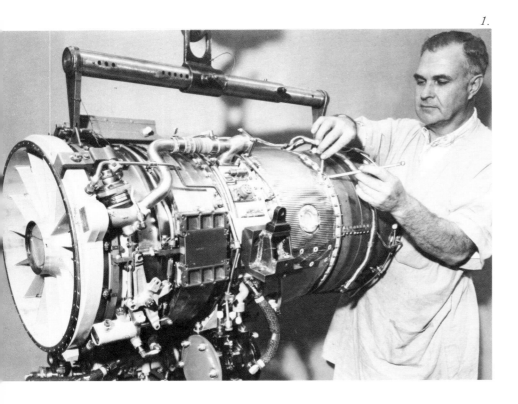

3.

1. Dry J85 in assembly.
2. Fred MacFee.
3. J85 flight test at Edwards AFB on F-102.
4. J85 afterburning turbojet.

2.

The challenges of translating the technology of "large" gas turbines into an engine of the size of the J85 were to prove significant. The Air Force had selected the "middle" engine—a conservative choice—and the Lynn engineering team spent several years attempting to make the new engine achieve its performance rating, including making substantial compressor and turbine section changes. The engine was particularly stall-prone. Fred MacFee, by then assigned to the J85 project, and his team determined that an engine start problem when the GAM-72 was dropped from the bomb bay of the B-52 was actually caused by the air currents within the bay of the giant bomber. The aircraft's air stream was turning the engine's compressor rotor in the reverse direction and the energy needed for starting was being used to stop the reverse rotation. The problem was soon remedied and the GAM-72s performed as promised.

The original design of the J85 for the GAM-72 was a "dry" (non-afterburning) engine. But Ed Woll, with his considerable afterburner experience dating to the 1940s and including the J35 and J47 engines, envisioned what the extra boost of an afterburner would do for the new little engine. Lynn engineers were soon experimenting with various J85 afterburner combinations.

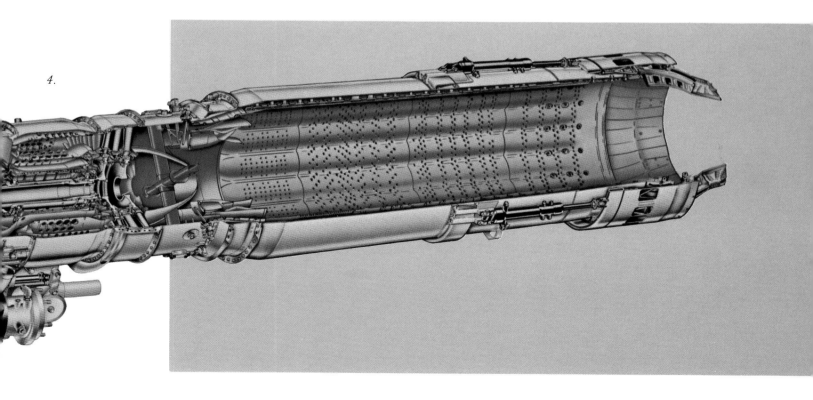

4.

THE FIFTIES

A new career for the J85

In California, Northrop Aircraft had been studying a small, lightweight fighter to meet what they believed were the requirements of both the U.S. and other nations for the 1950s and '60s. At the direction of the company's vice president of engineering, Ed Schmued, the Northrop designers had already conceived and constructed a mockup of the N-102 Fang, a single engine design, built around GE's J79. But the aircraft designers believed a twin engine airplane would provide greater safety and reliability margins.

Already aware of the dry J85's high thrust-to-weight ratio, Northrop asked Jim LaPierre to come to California and discuss the engine. LaPierre met with Schmued and Welko Gasich, Northrop's chief of preliminary design. The conclusion was that if GE could provide augmentation (afterburning) for the J85, its power would be increased as much as 40 percent and a twin engined version of their airplane could be designed around it.

1.

From this meeting came the N-156 powered by the J85-5, which was proposed to the USAF as a lightweight fighter. Although the Air Force saw no requirement at the time for this "little" airplane, they had been studying a replacement for the aging T-33 primary jet trainer. Northrop modified the design and the USAF selected what became the T-38 supersonic trainer. The difficult compressor and turbine problems that had plagued the early J85s nearly resulted in cancellation of the engine program. The Air Force gave Northrop and GE an ultimatum: fly the T-38 by April 11, 1959 or forget the J85 program. Ed Woll led a task force that had the J85-powered T-38 in the air on April 11th. More than 1,100 of the two-engined trainers were eventually produced and the now 20-year old airplane is still the primary advanced "school-room" for USAF pilots as well as a "showcase" airplane used by the Air Force Thunderbirds demonstration flying team.

1. *Northrop N-102 Fang mockup (J79).*
2. *First Northrop J85-powered T-38 Talon with flight test chief, Lew Nelson.*
3. *Kenneth Bush.*
4. *Canadian Air Force CF-5 (J85).*
5. *USAF F-5 Freedom Fighters (J85).*

2.

In the late 1950s the U.S. government, recognizing the need for a high performance, low cost air combat fighter that could be supplied to allied nations under the Military Assistance Program, chose the original fighter version of the Northrop aircraft. It was designated the F-5 Freedom Fighter. Sister ship of the T-38, the F-5 was built around two afterburning J85s, each producing 3,850 pounds of thrust. Less than four months after the T-38's first flight, the J85-powered N-156F—prototype for the F-5—made its first flight on July 30, 1959.

The F-5 became the "standard" air defense aircraft for more than 25 nations around the world during the 1960s and 1970s. By the end of the decade of the '70s, more than 12,000 General Electric J85s had been produced—primarily for the T-38 and F-5 family of aircraft. Lynn production under the direction of Ken Bush had once again achieved the rates of the "old days" of the '40s and the J85 rivalled the J79 as the "most produced" GE aircraft gas turbine.

In the late 1950s two major derivatives of the J85 were conceived—both for civil aviation use primarily in executive jet aircraft. The CJ610, a commercialized dry J85, and the CF700, a J85 with a fan added for higher thrust, traced directly to the increased emphasis that division management had placed on the civil aviation side in the middle '50s.

3.

4.

5.

THE FIFTIES

T58 bigger brother is conceived

Not long after the Parker/Woll team took over the Small Aircraft Engine department and the redesigned T58 had been accepted by the Navy, they began to look at future Navy requirements for an even larger turboprop/turboshaft engine. The ground rules established were: lower specific fuel consumption than the T58; more than double the T58's horsepower rating; and a higher compressor pressure ratio. Design work was begun in 1954.

Denis Edkins, who worked in the '30s with Frank Whittle at Power Jets and emigrated to the U.S. from England after World War II, was responsible for the engine proposal to the Navy. The powerplant presented was in the 2,500 horsepower class. There was no specific application for an engine of this size at the time, but the Navy wisely recognized the need for a larger shaft engine for the future and awarded GE a four-year development contract for $58.5 million. The intent was to bring the new T64 engine along slowly, placing particular emphasis on the larger, higher pressure ratio compressor.

1.

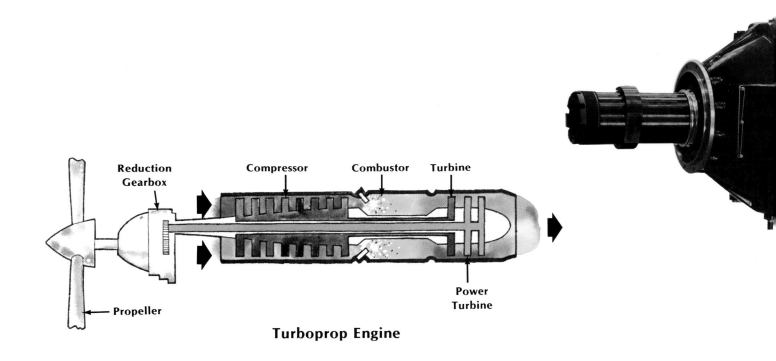

Turboprop Engine

Turboshaft Engine

The relatively leisurely pace of the development program, coupled with the fact that the engine had been conceived solely for the U.S. Navy, resulted in the Navy's taking an almost paternal interest in the T64. The powerplant experts in that service became an integral part of the engine's evolution.

Although the T64 project was created in the fall of 1957, it would be the early 1960s before this "big brother" of the T58 was selected to power any aircraft.

1. *Denis Edkins.*
2. *T64 turboprop engine.*
3. *T64 turboshaft engine.*
4. *Ed Burritt, Ed Woll and Waller Howard with T64 model.*

2.

3.

4.

111

Parker takes over: organization and products expand

On January 1,1955 Jack Parker was named general manager of the Aircraft Gas Turbine division after Jim LaPierre became executive vice president of the General Electric Company with his headquarters in New York. The dynamic, physically imposing (six foot-plus) Parker continued the expansion philosophy of his predecessor.

In April he named Gerhard Neumann to head the Jet Engine department with the charge: "You must never commit to do anything that you have any doubt that you can do." Neumann, in his first-ever general management assignment, accepted that philosophy as gospel and it served him—and GE's aircraft engine business—well during the decades of the '60s and '70s when, as a corporate Group Executive, he led the company's march toward world aviation gas turbine leadership.

1955 was the first joining of what later became known as the "Parker/Neumann team" that was to achieve major stature for aircraft engines in the nation's fourth largest industrial company. In a July, 1966, *Fortune* magazine story about GE's jet engine business, Jack Parker said that appointing Neumann was "one of the happiest decisions I ever made but a lot of people thought I had holes in my head at the time" (because of Neumann's lack of business management experience).

Neumann quickly put great emphasis on internal communications to assure prompt, accurate and open sharing of the department's business activities—and problems. Communications moved upward, downward and laterally in the organization. He began a technique that continued throughout his tenure as GE's top aircraft engine executive: "eyeball-to-eyeball" communications.

Neumann wanted to talk personally with every one of the by then 5,000-employee department. But no facility was large enough to hold that mass of people so he arranged for a series of what later became known as "Father Neumann's Tent Revival Meetings." Large circus tents were rented and set up in the Evendale parking lot, and—in a series of almost round-the-clock sessions—he exhorted his charges to go on to bigger and better achievements. Neumann established an internal management communication mechanism known as the "IoI" (Items of Interest) in which he required his direct reporting managers to inform him daily in a written document about the significant events of the past 24 hours. "No surprises" became a Neumann trademark. He put the identical requirement on himself: Neumann sent IoIs to Parker on the same basis. This Neumann-initiated management communications system is still used in the Aircraft Engine Group.

1.

As the business grew, the demand for additional technical talent became urgent. In one of the most concentrated recruiting efforts ever mounted within the company, Don Lester, under the direction of Marion Kellogg—who had been given division-wide recruiting responsibilities—established a requirement for 500 new engineers and 180 draftsmen. In 1956 a total of 622 new technical engineers were hired, many of whom were still with the company in the late 1970s. One of these was Brian H. Rowe on whose behalf Lester committed to the Immigration Service that he would not become a "public charge." Hindsight suggests that that was a very good bet.

Marion Kellogg, later reflecting on the growth in technological capability of GE's jet engine business, said, "In 1949 there were 92 engineers in the division and by the mid-'50s we had more than 2,000 engineers."

Although the intention of the reshaped Parker-led organization was to further expand GE's jet engine line, Neumann's first task was to examine and—jointly with Parker—ultimately discontinue one major new engine project. The X84 had been designed in the Flight Propulsion Laboratory department (previously Development department). After a lengthy session with many of the division's top engineers, the decision was made not to proceed with the X84 turbofan because of the technical risks involved. The USAF, already planning for the next-generation supersonic fighter bomber, was not happy with GE's decision since the X84 fitted their advanced requirements.

But another GE engine soon met those needs.

2.

1. *Jack S. Parker.*
2. *Joseph S. Alford and Parker review creative engineering program.*
3. *Neumann tent meeting, 1957.*

3.

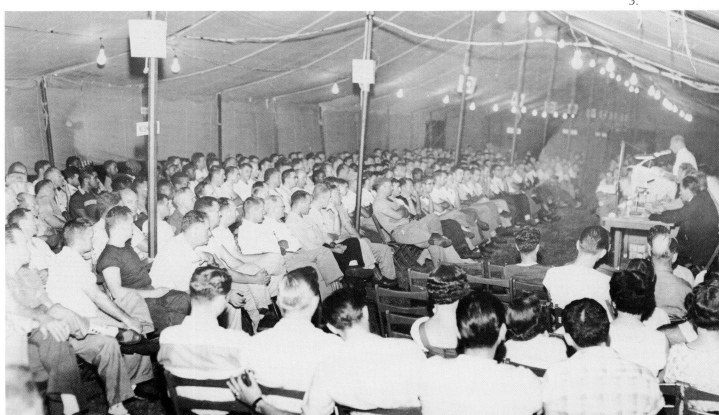

Mach 3 is in sight

North American Aviation in Los Angeles had been studying the USAF requirements for a new supersonic interceptor. In mid-1955 Neil Burgess, Ray Small and Jerry Pederson met over dinner with North American's Howard Evans and the J79-X275 was created for the interceptor study. The "275" meant Mach 2.75, but Gerhard Neumann suggested the engine could go to Mach 3. In early 1956 the engine design was presented to the USAF's Power Plant Laboratory. They were impressed but wary since they had already funded two Mach 2 engines, the Pratt & Whitney J91 and Allison J89, for the evolving interceptor as well as for a new bomber study, the WS-110.

The Allison engine had supposedly won the new powerplant competition, but the mission requirements for the new bomber were subsequently changed. Following a series of hardware demonstrations and basic design modifications to the GE Mach 3 engine, in May, 1957, the Air Force awarded

General Electric a contract to provide power for both the F-108 interceptor and the WS-110 (later XB-70) bomber, both to be built by North American. The engine was designated the J93.

The J93, the world's first engine designed to operate above three times the speed of sound, produced 27,200 pounds of thrust with afterburner and weighed 4,770 pounds. The first engine went on test in mid-September, 1958, and included many advanced technology achievements. Most significant was a new GE technique for electrolytically drilling longitudinal air cooling holes in the very large turbine blades. The process (STEM drilling) was utilized in subsequent company-developed engines.

Although the F-108 interceptor program was cancelled by the Air Force in the late 1950s, J93 development was continuing for the XB-70 as the decade of the '50s came to a close.

1.

Nuclear power for aircraft propulsion

In 1951 GE had been awarded a joint contract by the Atomic Energy Commission (AEC) and the U.S. Air Force to develop within five years sufficient data on nuclear materials and the shielding required in engine and airframe design in order to help the U.S. government determine if an atomic-powered aircraft was feasible. Roy Shoults originally headed the project. David Shaw was later the Aircraft Nuclear Propulsion department's (ANPD) general manager.

Considerable GE effort went into the program over the next several years. Pratt & Whitney, with a similar charter, was pursuing a parallel course. In 1954 the USAF identified a weapons system requirement for an atomic powered bomber, the WS-125. In 1955 GE was teamed with Convair and Pratt & Whitney with Lockheed in competitive airframe/engine development.

Within GE the nuclear power source work was being done in the supersecret Aircraft Nuclear Propulsion department. It was part of the Evendale complex, but carefully separated by its own security system. The actual gas turbine engine—or engines, to be exact, since the design called for two gas turbines coupled with one reactor source—was being developed in the Jet Engine department.

1. J93 (below) compared to J79.
2. STEM drilling for J93 turbine blades.
3. X211 nuclear engine.

2.

3.

The engine project, called the X211, was headed by Bruno Bruckmann, a stately and distinguished aircraft engine veteran. He had emigrated to the U.S. in the aftermath of World War II with the group of German scientists and technicians brought to Wright-Patterson Air Force Base in what was known as "Operation Paper Clip." Bruckmann had been vice president of engineering for the German aircraft engine manufacturer, Bavarian Motor Works (BMW), building jet engines during the war. Other members of "Paper Clip" included Hans von Ohain, Werner von Braun and Peter Kappus, later to become one of GE's foremost jet engine technical experts and a world leader in vertical takeoff and landing (VTOL) concepts.

The X211 was a giant of an engine—but relatively simple in concept. Gerhard Neumann, during his tenure with ANPD, had been instrumental in many of the designs leading to the ultimate solution. The twin engines linked to a single reactor had variable stator compressors and were straight turbojets with afterburners. The powerplant was 41 feet long and, with the afterburners, capable of producing 34,600 pounds of thrust.

By late 1956—despite the ongoing Convair/GE and Lockheed/P&W studies—the Air Force concluded that the WS-125 held little promise as an operational strategic aircraft. The aircraft program was discontinued. The engine studies were continued with no particular application targeted.

GE's X211 engine program was finally terminated in mid-1959 although there were several perturbations between 1956 and 1959, including conflicts with the Department of Defense over both available funding and the conventional-versus-nuclear powered strategic bomber.

What had been the world's largest aircraft gas turbine engine(s) was "officially" dead in 1961 when all funds for nuclear propulsion were eliminated from the U.S. defense budget.

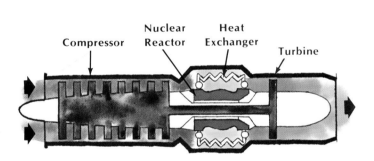

Nuclear Turbojet Engine

1.

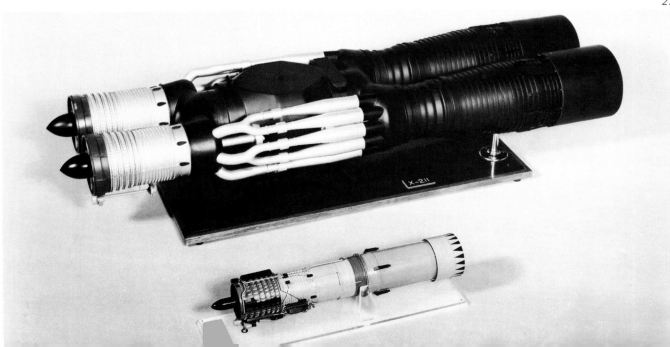

2.

GE enters jet transport market—late

The company had carefully tracked the evolution of the aircraft gas turbine for civil airline service as far back as the late 1940s. The J47 had been the first gas turbine certificated for commercial service by the Civil Aeronautics Administration in 1949 and several GE engineers had served on industry and government panels surveying the world jet transport market. But when Boeing and Douglas initially conceived the 707 and DC-8, no suitable GE engine was available and Pratt & Whitney's JT3, civil version of the J57, was selected by both aircraft companies.

P&W had been producing aircraft engines since World War I and was a prime supplier, along with Wright Aeronautical, of piston engines for airliners, but it had entered the postwar aircraft gas turbine field well behind GE as a result of the head start achieved by General Electric's leadership in development of military jet engines during the war years. The 707 and DC-8 selections enabled the veteran engine company not only to catch up, but to leapfrog in one giant step GE's position as the U.S. leader in jet engines.

The U.S. move into jet transports had been spurred by British competition. The Comet, although ill-fated because ample testing had not been done on the airframe, was flown in passenger service in the early 1950s. It represented the portent of the future for air travel.

To help motivate the U.S. aviation industry, one Pan American World Airways vice president in 1950 had sent to all of his aviation compatriots Christmas cards bearing a sketch of Boston's historic Old North Church with *three* lanterns hanging in the belfry. This time the British were coming not by land or by sea—but by air!

In 1955, with the J79 well under way in the development cycle, GE took steps to expand the already successful military jet engine business to include civil aviation.

1. Bruno Bruckmann.

2. X211 nuclear engine model compared with J79 engine.

3. Boeing 707 and

4. Douglas DC-8, both powered by P&W JT3.

3.

4.

117

Jack Parker, Ed Woll and Chap Walker surveyed both the U.S. and international air transportation markets and identified key airline management who would influence equipment decisions then and in the future. In the early 1950s a small Evendale product planning team of Vern Albert and Roger Boak began working with both airframe manufacturers and airlines to establish aircraft requirements.

The result of these efforts was the recognition that several airlines were interested in a "medium range" (shorter range than the already-designed 707 and DC-8 models) jet transport. Convair, which had been building 240, 340 and 440 piston-engined "medium" transports, wanted to develop such an airplane. And it appeared that a non-afterburning J79 would be the ideal engine for the Convair transport.

In April 1956 Convair announced the "Skylark," a four engine jet transport powered by a commercialized J79, the GE CJ805. General Electric, in its engine proposal to Convair, had not only presented a high performance, lightweight design, but it had also committed to develop a noise suppressor (everyone was aware jet engines were louder than piston engines) and thrust reverser (to help "brake" the high speed jet as it landed) for the CJ805. Jack Parker and Neil Burgess had worked closely with Convair management and engineers. With the commercialized J79, the "Skylark" was unveiled as the world's fastest jet transport. Burgess was named to head the newly created GE Commercial Engine operation.

1.

1. John B. Montgomery.
2. Convair Skylark (CJ805).
3. Convair 880 (CJ805).

2.

Within a month Trans World Airlines (which Howard Hughes then controlled) and Delta Air Lines announced the purchase of 30 and 10 respectively of the new Convair jet transports, by then renamed the 880 (to continue the Convair series of 240, 340, 440—and "double" the image of the twin piston-engined 440). The Howard Hughes role at TWA and in the selection of the 880 was to be a major factor in the ultimate course of the Convair program.

The original CJ805 engine had been specified at 10,400 pounds of thrust but the airlines and Convair soon recognized they would need more power and the rating was increased to 11,200 pounds.

Convair had received orders in 1957 for four 880s each from Brazilian and Argentinian airlines but the real push during that year was United Airlines, considered the keystone in the medium range market because of its broad and complex U.S. route structure.

Leader of the massive team effort to convince United of the merits of the GE-powered 880 for their route structure was retired U.S. Air Force Maj. Gen. John B. Montgomery. Montgomery came to GE in 1956 from American Airlines where he had been an operational vice president and in 1957 he replaced Jack Parker as general manager of the company's jet engine business when Parker was elevated to a corporate vice presidency in New York.

The forces competing for the United order—the P&W-powered Boeing 720 version of the 707—were not idle, however. Pratt & Whitney engines had served United well and reliably over the years.

3.

The GE/Convair forces were confident that the United order would open the floodgates for the 880. General Electric—at the urging of United technical experts—had leased a Douglas RB-66 and retrofitted it with CJ805s. Roy Pryor and crew were already flight testing the engine at the Edwards flight facility. In the pattern GE had established with the J79, the company intended to deliver a flight proven engine to Convair—in advance of the 880's flight.

Following a weekend decision-making board meeting in United's Chicago headquarters, Montgomery was waiting to meet with the airline's chief, William Patterson. As he waited, Montgomery checked the stock market ticker in the United office. On the ticker came the news that United had selected the Boeing 720.

United told GE: "You were untried." Airline experience of the competition had been difficult to overcome. GE still had a lot of catching up to do in the air transport business.

A major breakthrough came in 1958 when Swissair ordered a longer range version of the 880. The prestigious Swiss carrier's selection would make a significant impact on GE's future in civil aviation.

The CJ805-powered 880 first flew in the fall of 1958. But it would not enter airline service with TWA and Delta until nearly two years later. Howard Hughes, who considered that he had caused the 880 to happen with TWA's initial order for 30 airplanes, would maneuver to delay the entry of the 880 into passenger service until 1960.

1.

2.

A GE turbofan boosts civil prospects

The turbofan concept had been pioneered by Frank Whittle in the early 1940s and British Metropolitan Vickers had later built a rather complex fan engine based in part on a Whittle concept.

In 1956 GE became intrigued by a fan that could be added to an already fully developed jet engine. Peter Kappus, an outspoken proponent of the concept, believed that a large fan added to the rear of an engine would be both an uncomplicated and low cost method of: increasing the engine's takeoff thrust by 40 percent; lowering its specific fuel consumption by 15 percent; bettering its thrust output at altitude cruise conditions; and—as an added benefit that would later take on major significance—reducing the engine's noise level during takeoff and landing.

In the Flight Propulsion Laboratory department, a component development program, the X220, was created to demonstrate an aft fan concept. One great advantage to the aft fan was that it had no impact on the basic engine's operation. The engine, after all, ''didn't know what was going on behind it.''

Jack Parker saw to it that Gerhard Neumann's 1956 engineering budget included funds for the development of the aft fan concept and the J79-X220, later to become the CJ805-23, was born in that year.

The first full engine was tested the day after Christmas, December 26, 1957. A new turbofan engine had been created with relatively low development expenditure—and in a very short time. The CJ805-23 was the first U.S. turbofan engine and, in the 1960s, first in the world to enter airline service.

With the turbofan engine in hand, American Airlines became the next major target for a GE-powered jetliner. American had shown an interest in a GE engine in 1955 but the airline, working with Lockheed, had decided to pioneer gas turbine powered transports in the U.S. with the turboprop-powered Electra. General Electric, under Jim LaPierre's leadership, had decided in the early 1950s—despite considerable urging from several airlines, including American—that the future of air transportation was in the pure jet, *not* the turboprop. It was a prophetic business decision.

1. *John Montgomery, Gerhard Neumann, and Carl Anderson on CJ805/J79 line.*
2. *CJ805s installed on Douglas RB-66.*
3. *Peter Kappus.*

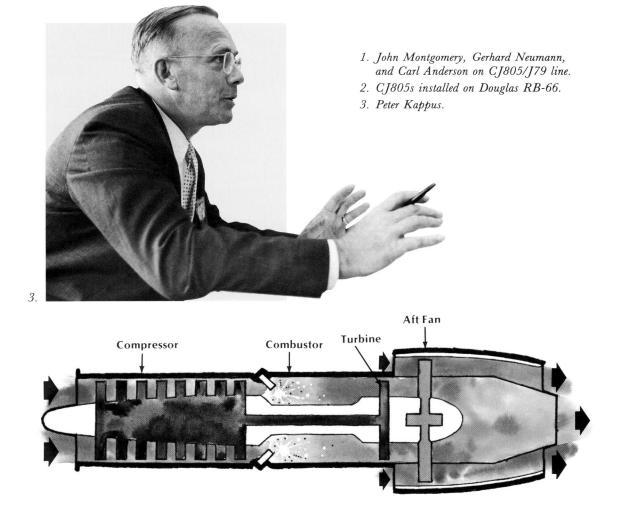

3.

Aft Turbofan Engine

Compressor — *Combustor* — *Turbine* — *Aft Fan*

American had originally shown interest in the 880 but, because the airline wanted a competitive edge, it had asked Convair to develop a larger—and faster—version of the airplane. From this request came the Convair 990 powered by four GE CJ805-23 turbofans—conceived as the world's fastest jetliner. Its design speed was Mach .91—just under the speed of sound.

American in 1958 ordered 25 of the unique airplanes. The 990 had four speed pods on its wings—devices resembling upside-down canoes that were derived from NACA's John Whitcomb's aerodynamic "area rule" concept to achieve the smooth movement of supersonic air over an airframe. Swissair changed its original order for five 880s to seven 990s. Howard Hughes, although already in the process of losing control of TWA, ordered thirteen 990s for that airline.

Even the U.S. Air Force entered the turbofan picture during this period. Parker, Montgomery and Burgess teamed to present the increased power, performance, fuel efficiency and lower noise levels of the new turbofan concept as a powerplant for the giant B-52 strategic bomber. Pratt & Whitney, heretofore a severe critic of the turbofan, quickly recognized that their important B-52/J57 application was in jeopardy. P&W designers promptly added a *front* fan to the J57 (an easier solution for them since the J57 was a dual rotor engine and the fan in front could be linked to the second rotor driving the forward section of the engine's compressor).

The B-52, of course, had originally been engineered for the J57 turbojet and, even with a fan on the front, the installation of the P&W engine was considerably easier than the pioneering GE turbofan. The Air Force went with the J57 fan retrofit of the B-52.

In one of his more laconic observations about the jet engine business, Jack Parker said, "We converted the heathen but the competitor sold the bibles!"

1.

A decade of expansion

The 1950s were expansive years for General Electric in the aircraft engine business. The company had entered into two wholly new markets—small engines and civil aviation. Major new facilities were in being. An organization designed to meet the burgeoning needs of the business had been created. Employment, particularly the technical staff, had been substantially increased. Bold, strong management had emerged who would guide the business for the next 20 years.

And, most important, a total of 15 new engines—more than in any other ten-year period in the company's history through 1979—had been created. Of the 15 engines originally developed in the decade of the '50s, eight were still in production in 1979.

1. *CJ805-powered Convair 990.*
2. *J47-powered Boeing B-47 and 1912 pusher aircraft.*

2.

The Sixties...decade of growth

THE SIXTIES

General Electric's jet engine business had flourished in the 1950s from the roots put down with the steam and gas turbines, the turbo-superchargers, the halting steps that led to the first U.S. jet powered flight, and the multi-branched turbine development that followed World War II. It had grown into a major business within the company. The relatively young Aircraft Gas Turbine division entered the '60s with assuredness and a feeling it could "take on the world."

Events of the first years of the decade would jolt that confidence and inspire some long, hard looks at exactly where the recently expanded jet engine business was heading. Even so, under the powerful, dynamic—and often unique—management style of Gerhard Neumann, the division would become one of ten major groups in General Electric by the end of the decade. Despite the difficulties the early '60s presented in both military and civil aviation, the late '60s would see the company in a stronger position in world aviation than ever before in its history.

1. *GE1 demonstrator: key to future growth.*
2. *Neil E. "Gene" Firestone.*

1.

Organization changes at the top

John Montgomery resigned in 1960 as vice president and general manager of the Aircraft Gas Turbine division, now renamed the Flight Propulsion division (FPD), to become president of Daystrom, Inc. He was replaced by Gene Firestone who had been a strong force in FPD manufacturing in the '50s during the enormous production buildup at the Evendale plant. But Firestone left GE in less than a year to become an operational vice president of International Telephone and Telegraph. In just under four years the division had experienced two top executives with quite different managerial styles. The fluidity at the top was reflected in the state of GE's jet engine business in the very early '60s.

2.

The next "big" engine

Although as the '60s began, the J79 and CJ805 were in full production (and the J93 was in development) at Evendale, GE management and forward planners were looking toward future military and civil requirements.

In 1959 the division had competed to provide the engine for a new USAF heavy transport, the Lockheed C-141 Starlifter. Edward E. Hood, who would become the head of GE's commercial aircraft engine business, was then working in preliminary design with Wally Bertaux and Wally Dodge. The team designed an aft fan transport engine based on GE's CJ805 fan experience for the Starlifter. Once again, however, the Air Force chose Pratt & Whitney's new fan version of the J57. Nevertheless, a small part of the foundation had been laid for GE's future large fan engine development.

At about the same time, then U.S. Secretary of Defense Robert S. MacNamara was trying to develop a single airplane that would meet the fighter and attack requirements of both the Air Force and Navy. The now famous TFX competition that produced the F-111 presented a golden opportunity for GE to develop the next "big" engine for the '60s and '70s.

In its March, 1963, issue, *Fortune* magazine headlined an article on the TFX competition "The Seven Billion Dollar Contract That Changed The Rules" and observed, "The engine competition for the TFX—the winner would walk away with a billion dollar contract in its hip pocket—was among three companies."

The eight original TFX airframe competitors were Boeing, Chance Vought, Douglas, General Dynamics/Convair (teamed with Grumman), Lockheed, McDonnell, North American and Republic. For the engine, Pratt & Whitney, counting on Navy support in the multi-service competition, was proposing the TF30—an engine developed under a $30-million USN program. Allison had reached a technical agreement with Rolls Royce and was proposing a version of the RR Spey engine. After originally submitting the J79 and not having it selected by any of the competing airframe companies, General Electric promptly came up with an entirely new design: the MF295, a dual rotor, front fan powerplant.

1.

2.

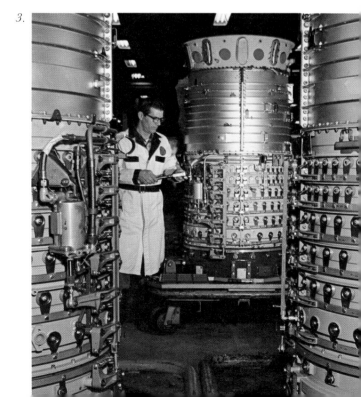

3.

The *Fortune* article said, "...the MF295 was several hundred pounds lighter than the Allison or Pratt & Whitney engine, and was smaller both in length and in diameter. This promised relief from the crushing limitation on weight, and it also permitted the narrow fuselage so critical to the Air Force's supersonic requirements." The magazine went on to state, "...word got back that the 'Air Force' was 'very high' on the MF295. Boeing, which had been designing the TFX around the heavier Pratt & Whitney for two and a half years...decided to switch to the MF295....Other contractors apparently shared Boeing's views for North American, McDonnell, Douglas, Lockheed—and indeed everyone except Republic, Chance Vought and General Dynamics/Convair/Grumman—eventually switched to the MF295."

GE had proposed the MF295 engine over the strong objections of a number of veteran engineers and some management within the company. The design represented two concepts—the dual rotor (as opposed to the variable stator) as a way of achieving increased compressor pressure ratio, and the front fan—both differing from GE design principles at the time. But a decision was made to press forward with the MF295 because Defense Department policy appeared to indicate that the TFX/F-111 would represent the entire next generation of first-line operational tactical aircraft for both the Air Force and Navy. Moreover, five airframe companies had specified the MF295 as their engine of choice.

After a lengthy series of evaluations by the joint selection groups of both U.S. military services, and with strong input from the Defense Department, the competition narrowed to two—the GE MF295-powered Boeing design and the P&W TF30-powered General Dynamics/Grumman design—and then settled on the General Dynamics airplane to be the new F-111.

Following the selection of the General Dynamics/Pratt & Whitney design, the Defense Department testified in extensive Senate Armed Services Committee hearings into the entire TFX decision-making and selection process to the effect that: "We see no difference between the two proposals so General Dynamics with the TF30 wins."

General Electric had been unsuccessful in a major military competition—one they believed they would win. But while it was no consolation at the time, the effort had not been wasted. Invaluable experience had been gained and it would prove a decisive factor in future competitions.

1. *Edward E. Hood.*
2. *Advanced combustor testing.*
3. *J79 production continues.*
4. *Proposed MF295 design for F-111.*

4.

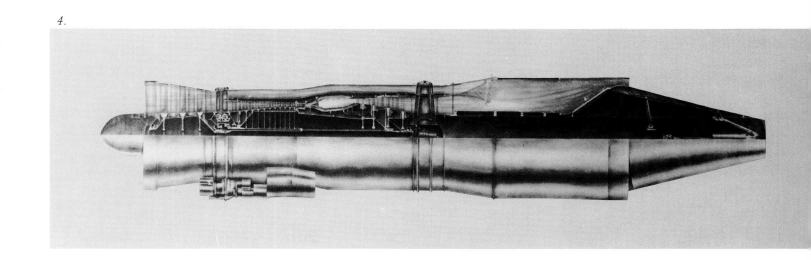

1.

1. *Gerhard Neumann.*
2. *CJ805-3 certification engine team.*
3. *CJ805-3 maintenance on-the-wing of 880.*
4. *CJ805-3 commercial engine with reverser and suppressor.*

Parker/Neumann team joined once more

Jim LaPierre retired as executive vice president of the company in 1964. Total General Electric business had expanded to the point where it became advisable to create five administrative "groups" representing the major segments of the company's business. Jack Parker was named vice president and group executive of Aerospace and Defense, in 1961.

In October, 1961, following Gene Firestone's departure to ITT, Parker selected Gerhard Neumann to head the Flight Propulsion division. With Parker as aerospace group executive and Neumann heading the aircraft engine division, the "Parker/Neumann team" was once again in being. In the waning months of 1961 another new era was to begin for GE's aircraft engine business.

Neumann assumed command of the Flight Propulsion division and was faced with immediate challenges. J79 production was down at the time because the USAF's F-104 requirements were lower than had been originally predicted and Air Force and Navy procurement of the McDonnell F-4 had not yet reached the high levels attained in the late '60s and '70s. Of the two applications for the J93, the North American F-108 had been terminated and the XB-70 had not yet flown. The X211 nuclear engine program had been cancelled. Ed Woll, who had succeeded Neumann as Small Aircraft Engine general manager, was striving to assure the future of the T58, T64 and J85 engines.

Most important, the CJ805 engine program for the Convair 880 and 990—General Electric's initial venture into the prestigious and expansive civil air transport field—was heading for trouble.

Commercial engines encounter rough air

The Convair 880 had not entered commercial passenger service until May, 1960, and sales of the jetliner were not even close to the original market projections of 257 aircraft over the life of the program. As *Fortune* magazine put it in a lengthy two-part story about General Dynamics and the 880/990 program in January and February, 1962, General Dynamics/Convair had become "entangled" with "the capricious Howard Hughes." The magazine quoted one GD executive: "The 880 was an advanced plane with a better engine than any other at the time [1956-59]. Hughes wanted to keep it from TWA's competitors. So people who might have bought the 880 if we [Convair] had been allowed to sell it to them, bought the DC-8 or 707 instead."

According to *Fortune*, when Hughes ordered the first 30 of the new Convair jet transport, there had been "an understanding [between Hughes and Convair] with Howard Hughes [that] had kept Convair from selling the 880 to anybody but TWA and Delta for a whole year." Because of this "understanding" and the loss of the United order, the market potential for the 880 had dropped to 80 airplanes.

The CJ805 for the 880 was GE's first experience with jet engines in airline service and there were reliability and maintenance problems to overcome. From this very challenging—and costly—experience emerged one of GE's basic business and design credos enunciated by Gerhard Neumann: "Do it right the first time...you're going to have it around for a long time to come." Neumann saw to it that the team of commercial engine designers, engineers and service and support personnel led by Bob Rowe followed up and fixed each and every CJ805 problem reported by airline customers. This dedication to supporting the product in service—despite the discouragingly small number of CJ805s built and sold and the company's loss on them of "about $90 million" as estimated by *Fortune* (July, 1966)—was to serve GE well in subsequent commercial transport marketing efforts in the later 1960s.

A TWA senior captain, asked in 1979 about the 880, said, "It was a good airplane with plenty of power. It was just too late."

2.

3.

4.

The Convair 990 did not fare any better than its older sister. After its initial flight in January, 1961, it was apparent the airplane was meeting neither its speed commitments to American nor its range specifications for Swissair. By September, 1962, Convair engineers had fixed the problems with help from GE Evendale aerodynamicist John Kutney who lived in San Diego for months as the engine nacelle housing the large fan engine was redesigned. But American, growing impatient with the delays, had reduced their 990 order, Swissair ordered no more of the airplane they had named the "Coronado" and a total of only 37 990s were ever sold.

A crisis occurred for GE on the CJ805 aft fan engine when it was discovered that the "bluckets" (the large two-section turbofan blades so nicknamed because they looked like a combination of compressor blade and turbine bucket) were cracking in airline service. GE ordered an immediate once-every-night inspection of the bluckets already installed in 990s and set to work to find the cause.

An investigating team was formed under John Pirtle, who was to head the company's work on the engine for the U.S. supersonic transport. Within a month the team believed they had found the cause of the cracking. Because they were not certain, they put an engine on test at Evendale under the same conditions encountered in airline service and predicted that blucket failure would occur at 9 p.m. on a certain Friday night. That was exactly what happened. Having pinpointed the cause, they made the fix and there were no more CJ805 turbofan blucket cracks.

When the problem was first discovered, the estimated cost to GE to redesign and replace all the bluckets in airline service was $13 million. Gerhard Neumann later introduced Pirtle to Jack Parker as "the man who saved the company $13 million."

1. Swissair 990 Coronado (CJ805-23).
2. John Kutney.
3. John Pirtle.
4. CJ805-23 "blucket."
5. Caravelle powered by two CJ805-23's.
6. Bob Rowe.

A bold international challenge

GE made one other bold move with the pioneering CJ805 turbofan for airline service. In 1961 the company purchased a twin jet Caravelle from France's Sud Aviation (now Aerospatiale), convinced that they could demonstrate superior airplane performance with the fan engine over the Caravelle's Rolls Royce Avon conventional turbojets. Douglas agreed to build and support the GE-powered Caravelle in the U.S.

Once again the now-seasoned airframe retrofitters at the company's Edwards Flight Test Center were called on to modify an airplane—this time a French jetliner—with GE engines. In the spring of 1961, following its debut at the biennial Paris Air Show, GE took the CJ805 turbofan-powered Caravelle—christened "Santa Maria" in honor of Columbus' caravel-rigged flagship—on a nine-country tour, putting on flight demonstrations for Swissair, Jugoslovenski Air Transport (JAT), KLM, SAS, Finnair, Austrian Airlines, Irish Air Lines, and Sud Aviation at Toulouse, France. The GE-powered Caravelle was the first jet transport ever to land in Yugoslavia.

In the U.S., TWA gave GE a letter contract for 25 Caravelles. American was also interested because of engine commonality with their fleet of 990s.

But financial negotiations with TWA ultimately failed; American joined with Eastern Air Lines to launch the Boeing 727; and the European carriers elected to stick with the original Avon-powered version of the Caravelle. Although it was unsuccessful in the short term, the bold move had helped pave the way for future domestic U.S. and international sales of GE commercial engines and it had provided the company with firsthand experience about jetliner engine installation, airframe modification and transport operations over actual airline routes.

The last CJ805 engine was shipped in 1962. M.R. "Bob" Rowe was manager of the commercial engine operation in the early '60s, guiding the inservice support of the CJ805. GE-powered 880s and 990s were still flying 18 years later with engine support provided by GE, and a 990 was used for many years as an astronomical observation aircraft by the National Aeronautics and Space Administration (NASA) Ames facility in Northern California.

But of greatest significance to the company's position in world aviation was GE's ability to demonstrate the credo, "Do it right the first time...you're going to have it around for a long time to come."

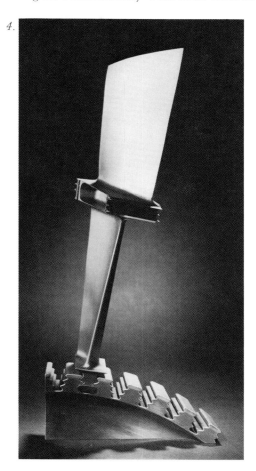

4.

5.

6.

THE SIXTIES

A time for advancing technology

The reorganization of the mid-1950s had established a Development department (later Flight Propulsion Laboratory department and then Advanced Engine Technology department) from which had emanated a number of significant breakthroughs in individual engine components, metallurgy, fuels, and techniques leading to advanced manufacturing processes. The GOL-1590 demonstrator for the J79 had been conceived in the development labs, for example. During this period—as part of the Evendale expansion and the move to provide company-owned facilities for increased efficiency and productivity in lieu of using government plants—GE had established a large complex devoted solely to the advancement and development of technology. The Evendale development labs for aircraft engine research became an extension of the company's Schenectady Engineering Lab and the Lynn Thomson Lab.

From this laboratory atmosphere came an engine demonstrator program—the X370—that provided GE with the technological base for developing direct lift engines and turbine cooling techniques that were later successfully applied to the large turbofan engines of the middle-to-late 1960s.

Wright Field's Propulsion Laboratory (the old Power Plant Lab)—and primarily Cliff Simpson and Weldon Worth—had established requirements for a very high thrust-to-weight ratio engine and turned to industry to meet them. As GE's Dayton office team of John Turner, Jim Micklos and Dave Jamison had done so often in the past—and would continue in the future—they provided liaison with the USAF's Propulsion Lab. The engine technology was intended as the next step beyond the J93 engine powering the XB-70.

1.

2.

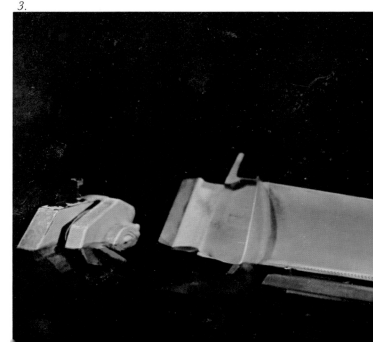

3.

John Blanton, who was to become one of General Electric's leading jet engine technical contributors and managers, took on the challenge. The Air Force wanted an engine with a ten-to-one thrust-to-weight ratio and a power capability to propel an airplane at three and a half times the speed of sound (Mach 3.5). They wanted to demonstrate, in addition, a very high temperature engine exhaust nozzle, an afterburner, and a Mach 4.5 ramjet.

When the complete X370 ran for the first time in July, 1961, it was the highest thrust-to-weight ratio turbojet in the world. Nick Constantine, with early GE experience in the Development department, had worked closely with the USAF technology requirements for this and subsequent advanced technology engines.

From the X370 demonstrator program came at least six different metalworking techniques that were still in production use in the 1970s, including electro-chemical machining and laser drilling. Cooling techniques permitting turbine temperatures as high as 4,000 degrees were pioneered on associated programs.

Another industry milestone was achieved by Blanton and his group when a successful engine demonstrator was designed and built using very advanced technology for use as a Direct Lift Demonstrator (DLD) engine in possible future vertical takeoff and landing (VTOL) aircraft. Both the X370 and DLD demonstrators, and their associated programs, while not resulting in contracts for development and production, provided major steps forward in technology of materials, processes and designs.

1. Laser drilling.
2. Advanced blade development.
3. Advanced electro-chemical machining.
4. John Blanton with Direct Lift Demonstrator.

4.

THE SIXTIES

Two worlds become one

When Gerhard Neumann assumed leadership of the Flight Propulsion division in late 1961, one of the things he knew he had to accomplish was the integration of two vastly dissimilar operations that were separated not only by a distance of 800 miles but also by philosophical and technical differences that frequently hindered the growth and progress of GE's aircraft engine business. A rivalry had developed over the years between Lynn—the ''mother chapter,'' so to speak—and Evendale—the ''offspring''—that had grown considerably larger than its parent. Neumann knew that rivalry well. He had served in both locations—at Lynn in the early days; later at Evendale in engine development, then as general manager of the Jet Engine department, and, immediately prior to taking over the division, as general manager of Small Aircraft Engines.

Neumann was very aware of what he called ''NIH (not invented here) factors'' that often resulted in the two locations competing directly with each other. To illustrate, Neumann recalled that when he was Evendale's Jet Engine department general manager pushing the J79, he sometimes found Ed Woll (then engineering manager of Lynn engines) ''proposing eight J85s for an airplane design while I was proposing two J79s.''

Recognition that GE's aircraft engines comprised one business serving essentially one set of customers—aircraft companies, the government, airlines and other civil operators—led to the ''one world'' concept that was to unify the business.

1.

2.

1. *J79 production at Evendale.*
2. *T58 production at Lynn.*
3. *Fan blade manufacturing.*
4. *Optical comparator.*
5. *Large broaching machine.*

Not long after he took over the division, Neumann began the process of centralizing the various functions that had been duplicated not only between Evendale and Lynn but often within the projects at each of the two principal locations. It would consolidate all manufacturing, engineering, quality, finance, employee relations and, of major significance, development and product planning functions, for the entire division. No longer, for example, would the production of all parts for small engines be located at Lynn or the satellite plants and the manufacture of all large engine parts be located exclusively at Evendale. If manufacturing of one type of component was more efficient at a specific plant, all parts of that type were produced there—whether their final destination was Lynn for small engines or Evendale for larger engines. The commonality of manufacture and the cross-fertilization of concepts finally achieved in 1966 resulted in substantial productivity increases that continued during the 1970s when GE concurrently had nineteen different gas turbine engines in production.

Organizationally the "one world" concept manifested itself in the so-called "project/function matrix." This organizational concept, while not original with GE, was pioneered at Lynn and Evendale in the '50s and later used by many aerospace and defense companies and government agencies. It established small, tightly knit "projects" to manage a given product line (such as the J79 or J85). Each separate project/product was supported by division-wide "functional" organizations (engineering, manufacturing, etc.) that assured the most effective utilization of manpower and facilities. Separate projects were purposely kept to the minimum staff necessary to manage a program. Functional organizations were permitted to expand to meet requirements.

3.

4.

5.

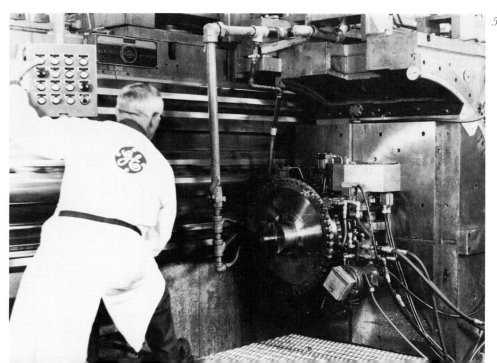

137

THE SIXTIES

Looking to the future—division-wide

As part of this reorganization of GE's "one world" aircraft gas turbine business, what had been separate product development and long range planning functions in Evendale and Lynn were joined. In October, 1962, the Advanced Product Planning operation (APPO) was created and in May, 1963, the Advanced Engine and Technology department (AETD) was established. From these forward-looking organizations eventually came the plans for GE's successful supersonic transport engine as well as the large turbofan engines that have provided the majority of the company's commercial aviation business in the '60s and '70s.

Jim Krebs, who headed a veteran team of gas turbine engineers in APPO, called for "...a better job of long range planning for the division...the identification of new product possibilities...[and] uncovering new requirements, fields of opportunity and specific applications [for GE engines]...." The APPO team included men who had already made lasting marks on GE's aircraft engine progress and would distinguish themselves even further in the future: Bill Rodenbaugh, Peter Kappus, Bruce Gordon, Jerry Pederson, Elmir Paulson and Bob Neitzel.

When the Advanced Engine and Technology department was created in the spring of 1963 to centralize all of the division's forward planning and development (including Evendale's Flight Propulsion Laboratory), Fred MacFee was named general manager. The move recognized the increasing complexity of the business and the small and larger powerplants being developed to meet civil, military, and emerging marine and industrial requirements.

1.

2.

3.

1. Jim Krebs.
2. Bill Rodenbaugh.
3. Elmir Paulson.
4. Jerry Pederson.
5. Bruce Gordon.
6. Bob Neitzel.
7. LM1500-powered Denison hydrofoil.
8. AGEH Plainview hydrofoil.

4.

5.

6.

New vistas opened for aircraft gas turbines

In late 1959, in a diversification move, the company studied non-aircraft applications of their aviation gas turbines—primarily because of General Electric's long experience with gas turbines as power sources for a variety of ground and marine uses. At Lynn the small T58 was adapted to industrial use for standby electrical power generation and for experimental hydrofoil boats. At Evendale the larger J79 was configured with a drive shaft and the company began working with Grumman Aircraft on Long Island, New York, on their new, large experimental hydrofoil boat, the Denison, for the U.S. Navy. In its marine configuration, the J79 was designated the LM1500. (GE's marine and industrial engines are designated by horsepower output—e.g., the LM1500 is in the 15,000 horsepower class; the LM100 in the 1,000 horsepower class, etc.)

The Denison and its LM1500 powerplant pioneered early hydrofoil development—although a number of companies in the U.S. and Europe were already working on the hydrofoil concept. The 100-ton, 60-knot development and demonstration vessel, launched in 1961, was the first large U.S. hydrofoil vessel and proved successful in its initial sea trials on Long Island Sound. GE's aircraft engine designers and installation engineers accumulated a wealth of knowledge about the marine environment—so different from the aerodynamics of the atmosphere in which they had been used to working. Later in the decade, the LM1500 was selected to power the U.S. Navy's new Patrol Gunboat (PGM) and 300-ton AGEH Plainview, a giant hydrofoil.

7.

8.

During the Navy negotiations for the Denison, the GE marine and industrial team of Bill Travers and Carl Villarreal learned of a Navy department study that led to one of GE's most unusual applications for an aircraft gas turbine.

All American Engineering of Dover, Delaware, had been given a contract to develop a portable ground catapult for launching Marine Corps jet aircraft. Similar in principle to the steam powered catapults used to launch aircraft from Navy carriers, the system was intended for use by the Marines in forward locations and it was to have the capability of being moved quickly by ground forces under battle conditions.

The GE team was excited by the new vistas this plan could open up and, working with All American, proposed the LM1500 (J79) as the primary source of power to operate the endless steel cable that would literally fling the high performance jets into the air. Using a retired factory prototype J79 gas generator modified to the LM1500 shaft configuration, the system went on test in 1963. Its success resulted in

GE's penetration of a new market for aircraft gas turbines and the establishment of a Marine and Industrial Products department. Because the ground launching system was frequently used for Marine Corps/McDonnell F-4s, one J79 (the LM1500) was in the position of catapulting two other J79s (power for the F-4) into flight.

Two veteran GE engineers were given responsibilities in the new product department. Ed Clark, with long GE experience in steam turbines for marine and industrial use, was named general manager and George Hardgrove, having risen in the aircraft engine ranks, was the department's engineering design manager.

During the 1960s this combination of GE steam turbine and aircraft gas turbine experience began to reap benefits as the LM1500 was selected for "peaking" (high usage hours) electrical power generation and additional marine uses for both primary power and boost for other hydrofoils. The LM1500 was also selected to provide power for long distance gas pipeline transmission systems.

1.

2.

GE gains fan experience—in a big way

General Electric had designed and developed the first U.S. turbofan aircraft engine (the CJ805), had created a unique-for-GE fan engine for the TFX (the MF295), and had demonstrated a 15:1 thrust-to-weight ratio lift engine (the DLD). The company was obviously in the "fan" business—and one development proved it in a big way.

In 1957 the company had been given a small study contract by the U.S. Army to look at vertical and short takeoff and landing (V/STOL) propulsion. From this small effort evolved a project that in essence caused GE to find itself in the airframe design business.

Working in Evendale's then Flight Propulsion Laboratory department, a team composed of Charlie Dibble, Morris Zipkin and a man who would become one of the nation's leading VTOL proponents, Peter Kappus, conceived a pioneering fan-in-wing concept for lifting airplanes vertically from the ground.

After the initial studies were complete, the Army asked GE to propose an airplane that would utilize the giant fans. The concept, promoted by Kappus and later by Art Adamson who would become one of the group's premier technical experts, called for two large wing fans plus one small fan in the nose, to be powered by conventional turbojets installed in the fuselage. Their exhaust (thrust) was ducted to drive the fans. The fans, running at high speed, would direct a column of air down toward the ground—and the airplane would lift into the air. After the vertical takeoff, the ducts would be rotated and the exhaust of the two turbojets would be directed to the rear for conventional aircraft flight.

One member of the design team who made a large contribution to the mechanical design of the lift fan was Brian Rowe who had come to the U.S. after extensive aircraft engine experience with deHavilland in Britain. Rowe would later head GE commercial engine business as well as serve as engineering vice president, prior to being named senior vice president and group executive for GE's engine business in 1979.

3.

4.

1. *LM1500/Denison contract signing (left to right) Carl Villarreal, Van Claxton, Bill Travers, and Herb Bass.*
2. *LM1500-powered catapult system.*
3. *Peter Kappus.*
4. *Art Adamson.*
5. *Brian Rowe.*

5.

141

The Lynn J85 turbojet was selected to provide the combination of conventional power and ducted thrust for the lift fans. The first system went on test in late 1959 and in early 1960 GE began working with airframe companies on an aircraft design for the unorthodox concept. The company collaborated with North American's Columbus, Ohio, group on aerodynamic models of the wing design and, after a series of tests in the NASA Ames wind tunnel in California, named Ryan Aeronautical of San Diego to build the airplane which was by then designated the XV-5A. Ryan selected Republic Aviation for the flight test program. The entire program was still under Army sponsorship. Art Adamson was the project manager.

Thus, the XV-5A had become one of the most unusual development combinations in American aviation history. The prime contractor for the airframe was an engine manufacturer; airframe work had been subcontracted by the engine systems developer to one aircraft manufacturer who, in turn, subcontracted flight test to another aircraft company; technology for the Army program had been advanced and tested by NASA; and the flight tests were to be conducted at Edwards Air Force Base.

After a series of design refinements in the early 1960s, a new tip-turbine driven fan system, now called cruise fan, was developed using an 80-inch fan driven by the more powerful J79 turbojet. The technical experience with this large fan (more than six and a half feet across) helped pave the way for later development of GE's high bypass ratio turbofans for the next generation of large transport aircraft. (The high bypass ratio expresses the relationship between the amount of air being pumped through the fan—and thus "bypassing" the basic compressor/combustor/turbine section— and the amount of air going through the basic engine.)

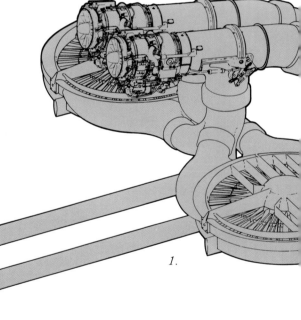

1.

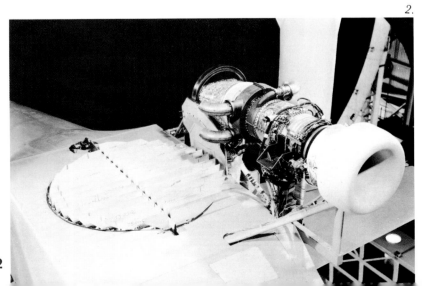

2.

Bob Goldsmith, who headed the lift fan program in the mid-1960s and who would become vice president of the Group's strategic planning organization, recalled a dramatic demonstration by one of America's most respected aerodynamicists that clearly spelled out to the GE team the need to solve some early development problems with the lift fan system.

GE had been having difficulty solving a problem with the exit louvers through which air not needed by the fan during takeoff is "dumped" from the basic aircraft powerplant. The XV-5A airframe designers believed the louvers were not sturdy enough to withstand the high pressure from the engine. Goldsmith recalls that John Stack, a longtime and highly respected NASA scientist who had joined the management of Republic Aviation, was a participant in a meeting called to discuss the problem. During the course of the discussion, Stack jumped up in exasperation, grabbed the venetian blinds in the office, rattled them noisily and said, "That's what's wrong with your louvers!" The GE team got the message—and stiffened the louvers.

3.

1. XV-5A lift fan system.
2. Lift fan system testing at NASA.
3. Bob Goldsmith.
4. Cruise fan testing (J79 and 80-inch fan).
5. Buildup of 80-inch fan.

4.

THE SIXTIES

With great anticipation, the GE "airframe/engine design team" gathered at the company's flight test facility at Edwards Air Force Base for the first XV-5A flight. After a series of careful system checks, rotating of the ducts from fan to conventional power, and basic engine runups, the aircraft was finally ready for its first attempt at lifting vertically from the concrete apron. The basic principle of direct lift is that the engine and lift system must produce more upward lift or pressure than the gross weight of the entire aircraft—or the plane cannot get off the ground.

With a Republic test pilot at the controls, full power was applied and the twin six-and-a-half feet fans came up to full speed, driven by the thrust generated from the powerful engines. The large airplane began to rise vertically off the apron as though lifted by a giant, invisible skyhook. It reached an altitude of several hundred feet, hovered in mid-air for nearly a minute (it felt like an hour to the anxious GE designers) and then gently settled back on the concrete. The lift fan system worked!

After several months of practicing the sequence of vertical lift and transition to conventional flight, the Republic test pilot had gained enough confidence in the aircraft and its lift system to give a dramatic demonstration of the XV-5A's unique capabilities. Without prior announcement to either GE or the Army, the pilot took off vertically, hovered at an altitude of about 30 feet, rotated the ducting for conventional flight, pointed the aircraft in a horizontal path across the California desert and proceeded to do a "barrel roll" (a complete rotation of the aircraft) within view of several very startled observers. When the only-one-of-its-kind XV-5A landed, the pilot faced some extremely irate program managers. But he had made the point: the XV-5A had demonstrated its unique capability for lift-off without any takeoff roll along with its ability to perform as a versatile conventional combat aircraft.

A second XV-5A was built and VTOL flight tests and demonstrations continued for ten years. Tragedy struck during that period when, in one flight demonstration, a Ryan test pilot apparently accidentally hit a cockpit switch that caused the airplane to prematurely shift from conventional flight to the hover mode. He lost control and was killed when the aircraft crashed.

Although VTOL technology had been demonstrated and delivered with the XV-5A program, action during the Vietnam War proved that the forward bases required for this type of vertical lift combat airplane were vulnerable to ground attack. The experience of Vietnam negated what had been the Army's plan for an aircraft that could both operate out of forward bases without airstrips and perform well in air combat against enemy airplanes. The XV-5A never reached the production stage.

1. GE lift fan-powered XV-5A in transition from vertical to horizontal flight.
2. NASA tests XV-5.

2.

1.

THE SIXTIES

An engine for all seasons

Not long after Gerhard Neumann had taken over the reins of the Flight Propulsion division in 1961, he conferred with Ed Woll and, with studies in hand of all of the present product line together with what they knew of future civil and military requirements, recognized there was a need for an engine sized somewhere between the J85 and the J79.

A study was initiated under the direction of Peter Kappus to determine just what size basic engine would best suit what the planners percieved as a broad range of potential applications. From this study emerged the "core" (or "building block") engine. Fred MacFee was brought from Lynn to Evendale and a task force was assembled under his direction to design and begin development of this core engine. It was designated the X101. The MacFee team included Kappus, Roy Pryor and Wally Bertaux for market planning plus an array of the division's top engine design talent, including Brian Rowe, who was later to head the Aircraft Engine Group, Bob Hawkins, Mel Bobo and Ben Koff, later to become the Group's chief engineer. The team had two objectives: (1) a detailed design for the new engine family; and (2) define the market potential.

The core ("building block") concept stemmed from the fact that a basic gas generator (compressor, combustor and turbine)—the "core" of all gas turbines—could be designed to produce a specified air flow and then used as a foundation for a variety of added components such as fans, afterburners, or thrust vectoring devices. Such combinations would more economically provide many performance levels and engine configurations tailored to specific aircraft requirements. The "building block" was born.

The MacFee team identified 30 different potential applications involving seven different types of new aircraft. The first building blocks had begun to take form.

1.

2.

3.

4.

5.

6.

The project for the new engine concept was established in February, 1962. When MacFee was named to head the new Advanced Engine Technology department, Jim Worsham took over the project. The engine was named the GE1 in recognition of its pioneering status.

The government initially supported the GE1 for a highly classified high altitude drone being developed by Ryan Aeronautical. From the GE1 core came the J97 for the Ryan drone—the first of what would become a long series of derivatives from the basic building block.

The division's GE1 helped spawn an entire family of development engines. GE1 technology was used in part to create the GE4 for the U.S. supersonic transport. The GE1/6 turbofan demonstrator begat the TF39 for the USAF C-5 transport. From the GE1/6 and TF39 lineage came the CF6 for the DC-10, 747 and A300 widebody transports. The GE1 "family" led to the GE9 engine for the USAF Advanced Manned Strategic Aircraft (AMSA). The GE9 later became the F101 for the Rockwell B-1 strategic bomber. And GE's TF34 and YJ101/F404 engines can trace their designs to GE1 technology.

The GE1 building block concept is perhaps the most significant business/technology achievement to date in General Electric's aircraft engine history.

1. *Fred MacFee.*
2. *Wally Bertaux.*
3. *Bob Hawkins.*
4. *Mel Bobo.*
5. *Ben Koff.*
6. *Jim Worsham.*
7. *GE1 demonstrator.*
8. *GE1 (top) compared with J47, same thrust class.*

7.

8.

The high bypass turbofan is born

The U.S. Air Force in 1962 had established Project Forecast to review and establish future USAF requirements and programs. General Bernard A. Schriever, heading the project, requested and received considerable industry data to supplement the military information gathered.

GE's data centered on the various fan programs—the XV-5A lift fan, the J79 and J85 cruise fans and the pioneering CJ805 jetliner turbofan—that the company believed could substantially improve thrust output and lower fuel consumption for the next generation of large aircraft. GE information was channeled to Project Forecast through Cliff Simpson in the USAF Propulsion Laboratory. From the study came a USAF requirement for the CXX large military transport with high bypass turbofan engines. USAF target date for the new transport was nearly ten years later—1972. With confidence in its fan experience, GE's management and engineers believed they could produce that engine right away.

A major reason for the company's confidence—and its motivation—was the fact that group executive Jack Parker had exhorted the division to "get going on the next transport engine and don't be overshadowed by the competition." GE's advanced planners already had under way a series of studies on turbofans including engines with very high bypass ratios.

The USAF encouraged GE to "put up or shut up:" submit an unsolicited proposal on the high bypass turbofan.

In what had by then become GE aircraft engine management practice, competing design teams were established in late 1963 to determine optimum engine specifications. By then the USAF, too, had established an engine design competition. The race was on.

1.

3.

2.

Within GE, a team headed by Don Berkey produced the winning design: an 8-to-1 bypass ratio fan, including a unique one-and-a-half stage fan (a full-size front fan plus an additional set of half-size fan blades) conceived by Lee Fischer, a very knowledgeable theorist and engineer who had contributed much to GE engines at both Lynn and Evendale. But it was just a paper design. In March, 1964, the USAF told GE, "You must have an engine running or you are out of the competition." (Pratt & Whitney, the other entry in the race, reportedly was in the process of demonstrating hardware for the CXX.)

With that message in hand, in his typical style, Gerhard Neumann turned on the heat.

Using the GE1 core engine as a basis (the building block concept was working well), the company laid out the design of the GE1/6 demonstrator: a turbofan engine with an 8-to-1 bypass ratio, a thrust output of 15,830 pounds and a specific fuel consumption (sfc) of only .336—a stunning reduction from the engines of the '40s that had sfc rates of more than one. The GE1/6 was one-half the size of the planned large transport engine but it did the job.

In one enterprising demonstration, the company ran the new development engine at full power for the benefit of an assistant secretary of the Air Force when he visited the Evendale plant to review progress on the program. He was convinced that GE not only had "an engine running," but had demonstrated the technological breakthrough of the high bypass turbofan principle. In retrospect most industry observers believe the high bypass turbofan represented a giant leap in aircraft gas turbine technology—an advance even greater than that of the first turbofans of the '50s over the original turbojets of the '40s.

1. *Don Berkey.*
2. *Lee Fischer.*
3. *GE1/6 team during first test cell run.*
4. *GE1/6 on test.*

4.

THE SIXTIES

Following the GE1/6 engine demonstration orchestrated by a team under the direction of Marty Hemsworth, the next step was to compile the formal proposal for the CXX's full-size engine. Clarence Danforth would lead the engine aerodynamics team. By then the Air Force had established a systems program office (SPO) at Wright Field for both engine and airframe management. The USAF requirements for technical, production and financial information to be included in the proposals for the airplane and its powerplants were awe-inspiring.

The GE engine proposal filled 90 volumes (and the company had to provide 50 copies of each volume). It demanded seven-day-a-week attention for three months (January-March, 1965) from the largest team of managers, engineers, technicians, writers, editors, draftsmen and production specialists ever assembled by the division for a single effort.

Gene Goedjen, the proposal manager, and Jerry Pederson, the technical editor, recalled that three days before the proposal was due, a request was made that additional volumes be assembled incorporating specific information from each of the 90 basic volumes for the use of specialized USAF evaluation teams. The largest auditorium in Evendale had been commandeered for the proposal effort and secretaries assigned to the task force spent one whole day moving through the aisles of the auditorium with supermarket carts gathering the proposal pages called for on their "shopping lists." The final GE proposal was delivered to Wright Field in a tractor-trailer.

Both airframe and engine for the new USAF transport were to be procured under the so-called "Charles Plan" of "total package procurement." The plan was conceived by then Assistant Secretary of the Air Force for Installations and Logistics Robert H. Charles. It called for contracting the procurement of the entire military system—development, production, all support systems, and operational service throughout the life of the program—at the inception of the project when the final decision was made on aircraft and engine makers. The contractors were betting high stakes at the outset on a program that could extend for more than ten years.

Oral presentations were required of all the competitors. GE's presentation was made in April, 1965, by a team composed of Jack Parker, Gerhard Neumann, Don Berkey, Jim Krebs, Marty Hemsworth and Dave Shaw. The company was taking no chances on this one. GE believed a significant segment of the future of the company's aircraft engine business was at stake.

1.

2.

1. *Marty Hemsworth.*
2. *Gene Goedjen.*
3. *Don Berkey signs TF39 contract; Paul Mosher, Jerry Pederson, Larry Steck, Bill Hess.*
4. *TF39 high bypass turbofan engine.*
5. *Clarence Danforth.*

In July of that year, project general manager Don Berkey was asked to sign a complex set of contracts, one set for each of the three potential airframe designs. Boeing, Douglas and Lockheed were the airframe competitors for what was to become the world's largest transport aircraft.

Because engine development has historically led airframe development (engines usually require a longer development cycle), in August, 1965, the Air Force announced—in advance of airframe selection—that General Electric had won the competition for the high bypass turbofan engine. In October the company was awarded a contract for $495,055,000 for the new TF39 engine—the largest single contract General Electric had ever received. GE was in the large transport engine business. And, as later events would prove, it was there to stay.

3.

4.

5.

151

The technology of the TF39 included many pioneering GE accomplishments: the 8-to-1 bypass ratio; a 25-to-1 compressor pressure ratio; a 2,500 degree turbine temperature (made possible by the turbine cooling techniques advanced from the J93); and a GE-designed thrust reverser (from CJ805 experience). The TF39's design, according to veteran GE engineers, contained nearly perfectly matched components—fan, compressor, combustor, turbine and exhaust nozzle. As a result of long years of component development in the company's Evendale and Lynn laboratories, each of the individual sections of the engine achieved significant efficiency improvements.

Late in 1965 the Air Force selected Lockheed to develop and build the world's largest jet transport, the C-5, at its Marietta, Georgia, facility. GE's Bob Harris had provided the important engine liaison with Lockheed. From this competition would come not only a fleet of military aircraft capable of moving the equipment for an entire Army division as well as providing airlift for tons of food, clothing and shelter needed anywhere in the world—but also the basis for the next generation of civil jet transports, the widebodied jetliners.

TF39 engine development and production proceeded during the balance of the 1960s and into the '70s with the normal challenges encountered when a pioneering engine of advanced technology is first fabricated, assembled, tested and manufactured.

In 1969, Bob Goldsmith was named to head the TF39 project. When TF39 production was completed in 1971, the company had built a total of 464 of the revolutionary high bypass turbofans—and the foundation had been laid for the company's next move into the subsonic civil jet transport market.

1.

2.

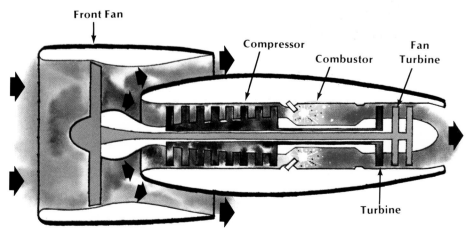

High Bypass Turbofan Engine

Front Fan

Compressor

Combustor

Fan Turbine

Turbine

1. *Lockheed C-5 Galaxy framed by TF39 engines.*

2. *Jim Worsham, Cliff Simpson (USAF), Don Berkey receive Goddard Award for TF39 development, 1968.*

3. *TF39 undergoing icing tests at Peebles site.*

The U.S. supersonic transport comes—and goes

With military supersonic flight a reality as early as the '50s, airframe designers and various U.S. government agencies soon had visions of airliners capable of carrying passengers faster than the speed of sound, traversing oceans and continents in less than half the time required by conventional airplanes. The military visualized the substantial logistics benefits to be derived from that same capability.

GE had proposed in 1958 a study engine called the X279M, a version of the J93 that powered the XB-70. Details of the Mach 3 class engine were provided to a number of airframe manufacturers for their supersonic transport studies. The X279M was very similar to the engine ultimately selected to power the U.S. SST.

The Air Force funded a development study based on their requirements. The X279M was one of the engines chosen. A number of aircraft companies designed supersonic military transports; Republic, for example, conceived a ten-engine giant. The designs that Boeing and Lockheed would eventually propose for the commercial supersonic transport had their beginnings during this time.

The British and French announced a joint venture to develop an SST, the Concorde, in the early 1960s. Both countries believed this bold move could reestablish their commercial aviation reputation in world markets—a reputation severely eroded by the success of the Boeing 707 and Douglas DC-8.

In 1963 during the biennial Paris Air Show, President John F. Kennedy called Najeeb Halaby, then adminstrator of the Federal Aviation Administration (FAA), proposing that he (Kennedy) announce that the U.S. was going to undertake the development of an SST. Halaby was to "feel out" principal American manufacturers about the project. Halaby talked with William Gwinn, chairman of United Aircraft (parent company of Pratt & Whitney) and apparently received a positive response. The FAA chief caught up with Gerhard Neumann at breakfast in a Paris hotel. Neumann, with five years of GE supersonic engine study experience in hand, reacted with characteristic enthusiasm.

During a May, 1963 speech at the U.S. Air Force Academy in Colorado Springs, President Kennedy made the announcement. The United States—already committed to sending a man to the moon by the end of the decade—would proceed with the development of an American SST.

1. *FAA Administrator Najeeb Halaby signs early SST engine contract with GE's George McTigue (left) and FAA's Gordon Bain.*

2. *GE4 SST engine on test at Peebles.*

3. *GE4 augmentor testing requires two J79s for power.*

1.

2.

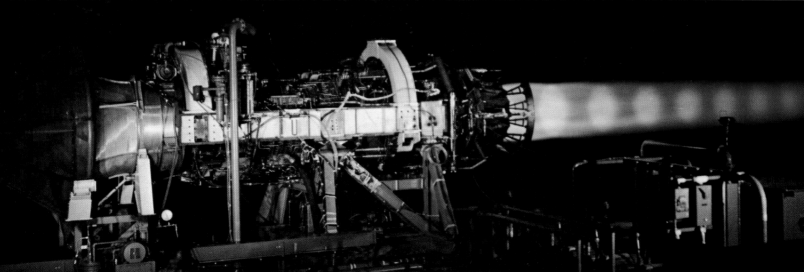

The FAA was named to manage the U.S. SST program and a special project office was established under Gordon Bain, who was succeeded by USAF Maj. Gen. Jewell ''Bill'' Maxwell and later Bill Magruder. Maxwell, a strong administrator, brought with him to the SST program the benefit of some five years of Air Force supersonic transport study and experimentation. The positive and aggressive Magruder provided the advantages of a test pilot background combined with commercial airplane experience. Each in his own way helped shape the direction of the extensive government effort. When the U.S. Department of Transportation was established in 1967, the SST program became part of that cabinet-level organization.

The competitors for the prestigious airframe contract were Boeing and Lockheed; traditional rivals Pratt & Whitney and General Electric were matched for the engine. In a July, 1966, article about the SST competition, *Fortune* said the ''prize'' to the winner of the engine race ''over a span of years may amount to sales of more than $4 billion...and immensely more in experience and prestige.''

The GE SST project was established in 1963 with Ed Hood, who for a time in 1962 had been, in his words, ''a one-man band'' on SST studies, as its general manager. Hood was backed by a core of veterans from the J79, J93, and TF39 fields of battle—Krebs, Pederson, Rodenbaugh, Pryor, plus Bruce Gordon, John Melzer, Dick Hevener, Nick Carter, Dick Smith, and Dave Moss. Walt Cronin would work with the Boeing SST aircraft team; Ed Silber would provide liaison with Lockheed. The engine was designated GE4.

3.

The 1966 *Fortune* story aptly described the competition: "The rival engines differ from each other almost as radically as the Boeing and Lockheed airframes. [Boeing was working on a variable, swept-wing design, while Lockheed's was a fixed delta wing.] The GE engine is essentially a more powerful version of the J93, which it designed for the XB-70 bomber, presently being flight tested in Southern California. It is a straight jet with an afterburner, a standard device long used on fighters to reignite exhaust gases when the plane needs extra thrust. The main innovations are concentrated in techniques for cooling the turbine blades to permit unprecedented turbine inlet temperatures (up to 2,300 degrees, as against 1,800 degrees in today's jets).

"P&W's entry will be a fan-jet engine that supplements its exhaust thrust with a fan, operating much like a propeller, to accelerate air passing around the outside of the engine. Instead of an afterburner, P&W proposed to employ an advanced technique called duct burning, by which air from that fan is fed into ducts guided into the tail pipe when extra power is needed. P&W argues that its fan-jet design will make the engine quieter and more efficient in subsonic flight—during holding delays at airports, for example. GE maintains that its engine will be more efficient at high speeds, and that its reliability in principle has already been proved by XB-70 experience. Also GE's engine will cost less, reportedly about $1,100,000 versus $1,400,000 for the P&W contender."

With the GE4 design established and work under way to build the first prototype engine, the biggest challenge for the General Electric team was to convince U.S. government officials who would make the final airframe and engine decisions—and the American and overseas airlines who would heavily influence the decision—that the GE entry was superior. The airlines represented a formidable hurdle.

Many of them thought of General Electric only in association with light bulbs, kitchen appliances and electrical power generation. The balance recalled the relatively recent 880/990 jetliner experience.

1.

2.

The formal engine proposals to the government were due in September, 1966 (Labor Day weekend) and a decision on the winners was scheduled for December 31 that year.

Benefitting from the overwhelming experience of the massive C-5/TF39 proposal effort, the FAA limited the formal SST proposals to 3,000 pages. It was little more than a year since the 90-volume TF39 proposal had consumed three full months in the lives of several hundred GE technicians. A 3,000-page proposal would be a ''piece of cake''—they thought. When the edited proposal was finally printed, it numbered 3,600 pages. Undaunted, the team simply cut out 600 pages, adding a notice at the end of the proposal that stated: ''Extensive additional material is available on request.'' The government evaluation team requested the additional material.

Boeing and General Electric each ended 1966 with a bang! On December 31, the Mach 2.7 GE4-powered Boeing 2707 was selected by the U.S. government as the winner of the American supersonic transport competition.

The General Electric team had achieved its objective: all but two U.S. airlines had voiced a preference for the GE4; the majority of overseas carriers voted for the GE engine; Boeing had proposed the 2707 with the GE4 as the preferred powerplant; and the U.S. government evaluation team had ultimately selected the GE4.

1. *GE4 testing with Boeing nacelle.*
2. *Fred Garry with GE4 during buildup.*
3. *John Pirtle and GE4 ready for test.*

3.

Development of the prototype began in 1967 under the leadership of John Pirtle and his engineering team. The engine was demonstrated both in Evendale test cells and at the company's outdoor test site located in the rolling hills of southeastern Ohio near the town of Peebles. As part of its policy of investing company funds in privately-owned facilities, GE had acquired and outfitted the Peebles site in the late 1950s in anticipation of requirements for outdoor, remote testing of future large engine systems as well as for rocket engine testing. A dual-cell altitude test facility, capable of testing the SST engine at conditions up to 80,000 feet altitude and Mach 3 speeds, was built at the Evendale plant.

The GE4 was the most powerful turbojet in the world—producing 69,900 pounds of thrust, enough power to illuminate one million 100-watt light bulbs. The engine, scaled up from the GE1 and relying heavily on J93 aerodynamic design, pioneered the use of hollow compressor blades (to save weight in the giant powerplant); was fitted with the largest afterburner ever built; and utilized turbine cooling techniques derived from X370 and TF39 experience.

In 1970 and 1971 a nationwide campaign was mounted warning of the dangers to the earth's environment of SST operation. Following a series of debates arguing both sides of the issue in public forums, on television and on the editorial pages of almost every newspaper and magazine in America, on March 29, 1971, the U.S. Senate—by a vote of 49 to 48—cancelled the American SST program. Nine years later, the earlier-vintage British/French Concorde continued to operate in passenger service across the North Atlantic and from Europe to the Middle East.

1.

B-70—and J93—program terminated

The J93 engine that had provided the basic technology for the SST powerplant as well as turbine cooling techniques and manufacturing advances for a host of other engines, including the TF39, was delivered to the Air Force and installed in the North American XB-70 by mid-1962. Bruno Bruckmann had moved from the X211 to become J93 project manager. Both engine and airframe programs were progressing smoothly.

In September, 1964, the revolutionary three-times-the-speed-of-sound bomber lifted off the Edwards Air Force Base runway for the first time. The XB-70 looked very much like a praying mantis as it hunched on its massive landing gear, poised with drooped nose to leap into the sky. The airplane's inlet ducts that fed air to the six powerful J93s had the appearance of long, mysterious tunnels.

Two XB-70s were built and, although the flight demonstration program was proceeding as planned, one of the experimental bombers was lost. The accident occurred when an F-104 flying "chase" collided with the XB-70 in mid-air.

The XB-70 had demonstrated its Mach 3 cruise capability by October, 1965. But by then U.S. long range strategic defense requirements had changed. The Department of Defense terminated the program in the early 1960s.

Design studies were begun that eventually led to the B-1 bomber. But the XB-70 and J93 engine had succeeded in significantly advancing the technology required for high speed, high altitude, long range flight.

1. Boeing 2707 SST.
2. J93 unveiling, 1963, Washington, D.C.
3. North American XB-70 (J93).
4. Bruno Bruckmann (left) and Ed Hood compare J93 (above) with GE4.

THE SIXTIES

"One world" becomes even stronger

The integration and centralization of GE's aircraft engine business had begun in 1961. Lynn and Evendale, together with the satellite manufacturing plants in Massachusetts, Vermont, New Hampshire and New Mexico, had been carefully molded into a single, smoothly functioning business. The Flight Propulsion division's product lines—whether physically located at Evendale or Lynn—fitted neatly into three categories: commercial, military, or marine and industrial. They were supported by the functional and staff organizations, and it was clear the project/functional matrix concept provided a more efficient and productive organization.

By 1966 the volume of sales and the breadth of GE's engine product line had grown to such an extent that a further organizational step forward was necessary. The stature of the jet engine business was given recognition in two reorganization moves—one in March, 1966, the other in January, 1968.

The 1966 organizational move created several new entities: a military engine program department with Ed Woll as general manager; an operations department headed by Dave Shaw, responsible for all division manufacturing, product support and the growing marine and industrial business; and a division-wide engineering organization under Fred MacFee, responsible for functional technical support of all programs as well as for the development of advanced engines, including the embryonic commercial engine ventures.

On January 1, 1968, General Electric announced a realignment of its entire corporate structure that recognized the growth potential of the company's overall business. Ten "Groups" were created, each representing one of the major GE business segments. The company's jet engine business was one of those major segments. The Flight Propulsion division became the Aircraft Engine Group. Gerhard Neumann was named vice president and group executive. The ten Groups reported directly to the office of the chairman of the company, Fred Borch. The office of the chairman consisted of Borch and three vice chairmen, including Jack Parker. The Parker/Neumann team had taken another step forward.

Ed Woll became Military Engine division vice president; Ed Hood was named vice president of the Commercial Engine division; Ray Small was named general manager of the Aircraft Engine Support and Service division, which included the marine and industrial business; Fred MacFee was made vice president of the Aircraft Engine Operating division; Fred Garry became vice president of the Aircraft Engine Technical division; and the Group's legal, financial and business planning support functions were headed by Jim Sack, Tex McClary and Lou Schmidt, respectively.

2.

Another opportunity for a bold move

GE's success in the C-5/TF39 competition gained the company the opportunity necessary to re-establish itself in commercial aviation. Despite the 880/990 experience, many of the world's airlines had given GE engine technology a vote of confidence as the SST competition unfolded. Most important, the world aviation industry anticipated that development of the USAF C-5 transport program would surely lead to development of an airplane for the next generation of air travelers. The winners of that competition—Lockheed and GE—would almost certainly have a leg up on the market for that airplane.

Boeing and P&W had other ideas. Boeing modified their C-5 proposal for airline use, making the new airplane smaller but faster than the USAF transport. P&W completely revamped their turbofan engine entry into a larger, higher thrust powerplant. General Electric knew there would be stiff competition for this next round of airline engine business but believed the TF39—already well along in development—offered significant advantages over P&W's new proposal.

1. David F. Shaw.
2. Gerhard Neumann, (seated, right) and Aircraft Engine Group staff, 1968.
3. Lockheed C-5A Galaxy on first flight.
4. Lockheed C-5A (TF39).

161

As they had done with the original round of American jetliners, Pan American World Airways set off the next major phase in the evolution of jet transports. Although many believed the so-called "jumbo" jet would be an airplane for the late 1970s and 1980s, Pan Am wanted the new, revolutionary aircraft to enter service much more quickly. Boeing responded with appropriate speed: both GE and P&W were asked to furnish technical data, price and delivery proposals for the Boeing jumbo jet.

The Pan Am-influenced airplane specifications called for significant speed increase at cruise altitudes of 35,000-40,000 feet. GE proposed a commercialized version of the TF39, the CTF39, and, although the basic engine was well-suited for the C-5, it could not quite meet the Pan Am requirements for the Boeing airplane. A GE engine for the Boeing airplane, by now named the 747, would have to be about 10 percent larger and that meant a separate—and costly—development program from the TF39 effort.

Following an intensive series of soul-searching GE management sessions, the company made a momentous decision: it would withdraw from the 747 competition. The decision was made because the division's management was convinced a new and separate development effort for a program of the magnitude of the 747 could inflict a crippling drain on resources and thus impinge on the continuing success of the TF39 program. GE "walked away" from the 747 competition and all its potential. Pan Am ordered the P&W-powered Boeing 747 and the widebody jetliner era was off and running.

1.

2.

1. Gerhard Neumann and Ed Hood with CF6 model.
2. CF6-6 turbofan trimetric.

Both Douglas and Lockheed had, of course, been working with domestic and international airlines to determine the carriers' requirements for the next generation of air transports. American had defined a twin-engine "airbus" for the Chicago-Los Angeles type of route. And another competitor had entered the engine picture. Rolls Royce was developing the RB211 turbofan which joined GE's commercial TF39 and P&W's JT9 in vying for the next round of engine orders.

Although the company had withdrawn from the 747 competition, Jack Parker and Gerhard Neumann knew that GE must pursue development of a commercial turbofan. In 1967 a Commercial Engine Projects operation was created with Ed Hood as its manager. It included the SST engine, CJ805 product support, the CJ610 and CF700 engines for business jets, and a new engine project, the CF6, under the direction of Brian Rowe. Art Adamson returned from Lynn to head CF6 engine development.

General Electric teams, including field sales veterans Jack Armstrong, Phil Myers, Bob Harris, Ed Silber, Vern Albert, Bill Travers, Ron Krape, Walt Cronin, Ad Fioretti, Tom Bergmann, and Walt Disney began meeting with airframe manufacturers and the airlines to discuss the CF6, a smaller derivative of the TF39 (and an extension of the GE1 building block concept). On the basis of their joint studies with the three engine makers—and particularly GE with its CF6—Douglas and Lockheed evolved widebody aircraft that were smaller than the 747, were designed to serve high density, medium-range routes, and were powered by not two but three turbofans. The Lockheed L-1011 and the Douglas DC-10 emerged as the newest competitors in the widebody race.

Lockheed moved quickly into the marketplace with the L-1011. Spirited competition ensued when Douglas entered with the DC-10. Both airplanes were being studied with the new GE, P&W and RR turbofans. The multiple engine offerings created an entirely different atmosphere from the traditional climate of the past when an airplane was designed around a single engine type and the buyer had no choice. For the first time the airlines found themselves in a position to voice their own technical, service, support and financial requirements as these factors affected engine selection.

In February, 1968, American kicked off three-engine widebody sales when they selected the DC-10—but without an engine specified. Lockheed was immersed in tense negotiations with TWA, Eastern Air Lines and Delta Air Lines—involving particularly these carriers' L-1011 engine choice. Both GE and RR were modifying engine specifications and economic considerations almost weekly to meet changing conditions and requirements. In late March, 1968, the three airlines made their decision to buy the Rolls Royce-powered L-1011. It was a black day in Evendale and Lynn.

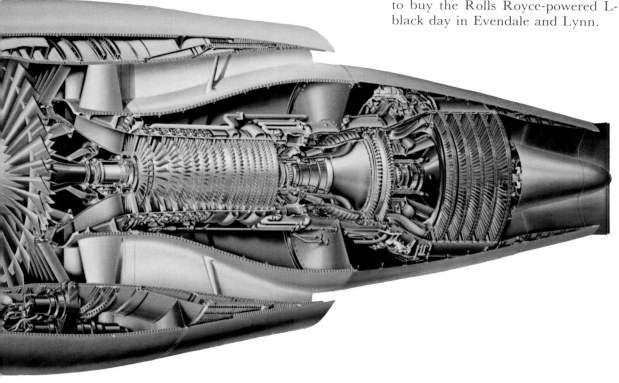

THE SIXTIES

All was not lost

American had already ordered the DC-10—but no engine had been selected. And United Airlines had not yet made a decision. These two airlines were the key to the future of the airplane—and to GE's new CF6. Although United's late-1950s selection of a Boeing 707-720 plane had been a major factor in the ultimate fate of the Convair 880/990 program and its GE CJ805 engines, the airline became convinced the CF6 would be a reliable, efficient engine in airline service—and that GE had gained valuable experience from the CJ805 program. United selected the GE-powered DC-10 in April 1968; American did likewise. The CF6 was launched with two prestigious U.S. carriers whose routes the DC-10 matched ideally.

National Airlines soon followed suit and the next target was the European carriers, particularly the KSSU group—KLM, Swissair, SAS and the French carrier, UTA (Union de Transports Aeriens). The KSSU group wanted an airplane with longer range than the one ordered by the U.S. carriers. That meant a higher thrust engine.

The original CF6, the engine that had been seriously considered in the first months of the widebody competition, was designed to produce 32,000 pounds of thrust. That power level had been ideal for the initially proposed three-engined Douglas and Lockheed aircraft. But it is an historic fact of aviation that airplanes traditionally grow larger—and power requirements increase—as users demand longer range, higher speeds and greater carrying capacity. With more than 20 years of jet engine design, development and operational experience behind them when initial plans for GE's new generation of engines (the GE1 family) were laid out in the early 1960s, the company's designers had taken into account that truism of airplane design. The CF6 design adequately provided for growth. Major contributors to this effort by the Rowe-headed project team included Art Adamson, Herb Garten, Bob Smuland, Ted Stirgwolt and Ron Welsch.

1. *United Airlines DC-10 series 10 (CF6-6).*
2. *American Airlines DC-10 series 10 (CF6-6).*
3. *CF6-50 turbofan engine.*
4. *Airbus Industrie A300 (CF6-50).*
5. *KSSU and ATLAS airline logos.*

1.

2.

Basic CF6-6 power output had been increased to 36,000 pounds; later to 40,000 pounds of thrust. But that was still too low for the airplane required by the KSSU group. The GE team recognized it would take 50,000 pounds of thrust to win. From the KSSU challenge emerged the CF6-50, an engine in the 49,000-54,000 pound thrust class. The longer range DC-10 was selected by KSSU and the decision was announced during the 1969 Paris Air Show. Countless toasts with fine champagne were proffered in Paris the evening of the victory. General Electric had taken another step in its bold reentry into the big time world of international commercial aviation.

A significant factor in the KSSU decision to go with GE engines for the DC-10 had been the confidence exhibited by Swissair, a respected international airline, in General Electric's ability to deliver what was promised—and to provide "over and above" service to the airlines during the operational life of the engine. Swissair's confidence was engendered by their experience with the GE-powered Convair 990 Coronado, an airplane that had served them well.

The KSSU success was quickly followed by another major European breakthrough. The longer range, more powerful GE-engined DC-10 was now a reality and the second large European airline consortium, ATLAS (Alitalia, Iberia, Lufthansa, Air France, Sabena), chose the same basic airplane as the KSSU group. A domino effect was beginning, as more world airlines selected the DC-10.

Both the DC-10 and the L-1011 had originally been called "airbuses" but that generic nickname faded early following the growth of the two airplanes and their change from two to three engines. But the basic "airbus" idea—a somewhat shorter range twin jet with a wide fuselage for greater passenger capacity—was still alive in Europe. France's Sud Aviation and Germany's VFW Fokker, later joined by Britain's Hawker Siddeley, were studying a European airbus. The creation of GE's CF6-50 was very attractive since it offered plenty of power for the twin engine airplane; eight European airlines had already selected the engine, assuring commonality and operational service on the Continent; and a total powerplant/nacelle package had been proposed to the newly created joint venture company, now called Airbus Industrie. The American company, Rohr Industries, was to build the complete nacelle, including total engine installation, for the CF6-50-powered DC-10. The same nacelle installation fitted almost exactly the European airbus requirements. In late 1969 the CF6-50 was selected to power the new Airbus Industrie A300.

General Electric's advanced turbofan for civil aviation was now powering three commercial jetliners: two separate models of the DC-10 and the A300.

3.

Airbus A300

4.

5.

Then the TF39/CF6 went to sea

In 1967-68 GE's marine and industrial programs were concentrated on the J79-derived LM1500 and the T58-derived LM100, but the small band of proponents for non-aircraft use of the company's gas turbine engines knew there was a requirement for larger and more efficient stationary powerplants. The development of the TF39 provided the basis for a new engine.

Bob Miles, who had helped steer the 1966-68 "one world" reorganization, was named general manager of the newly created Marine and Industrial department in January, 1968; the experienced George Hardgrove became manager of engineering for the next generation engine; and Jack Horning was project manager for a program called, at the time, the DX. The TF39 derivative for marine and industrial applications became the LM2500 (25,000 shaft horsepower). The DX project was created because the U.S. Navy was studying a new class of destroyer that called for 80,000 shaft horsepower to drive its high speed propellers.

The Navy in 1967 had launched a large cargo transport, the GTS Admiral William M. Callaghan, powered by two Pratt & Whitney FT4 marine engines. At a March, 1968, Washington, D.C. meeting with the Navy, the confident GE M&Iers proposed that one LM2500 be installed on the Callaghan to replace an FT4 and that a comparative evaluation be made by the Navy. The GE contingent even had the temerity to promise the Navy it could install in the Callaghan the first LM2500 built.

After a real scramble to construct and test the new engine that was designed around the basic gas generator and low power turbine of the TF39/CF6, the first LM2500 was installed in the Callaghan in 1969. The engine's performance met the promises made to the Navy by the enthusiastic GE team. After 25,000 hours of LM2500 operation on board the Callaghan, the second FT4 was replaced by another LM2500. The twin engine GE-powered Navy cargo transport continued to ply the North Atlantic through the 1970s.

1.

2.

4.

3.

The Callaghan experience, however, quickly reminded the GE engineers of a basic physics lesson: salt water is different from air. Accustomed to the relatively benign effects of the atmosphere on jet engines for airplanes (albeit accounting for the tortures of temperatures that often exceed 2,000 degrees), the engine builders had not made adequate provision to prevent the corroding and pitting of finely machined compressor and turbine blades caused by constant exposure to the sea.

After only 2,000 hours of operation across the North Atlantic, the LM2500's blades were seriously corroded. GE developed a resistant blade coating that solved the problem on the Callaghan—and all succeeding General Electric marine powerplants.

As the GE M&I contingent had intended when they brazenly proposed the first LM2500 Callaghan installation in 1968, its success had a major impact on the selection of power for the Navy's new DX destroyer. In late 1969 a veteran GE manager with extensive engineering and marketing experience was named to head the Marine and Industrial department. Sam Levine's specific business objective was to "win the Navy destroyer competition."

A year later, December, 1970, Litton chose the LM2500 to power the new DD-963 Spruance-class destroyer. The 7,600-ton Spruance-class destroyer was the Navy's first gas turbine-powered combat vessel; it was the largest naval surface ship program since World War II; and it represented perhaps the largest single ship propulsion contract in history. Each of the DD-963-class destroyers is powered by four 21,500 shaft horsepower LM2500s; the ship is capable of speeds in excess of 30 knots.

The 1960s had seen the emergence of General Electric into an entirely new aircraft-derived gas turbine business—first with the LM100 and LM1500 and later with the LM2500 for marine and industrial applications.

1. Bob Miles.
2. George Hardgrove.
3. Jack Horning.
4. LM2500 marine gas turbine.
5. GTS Admiral Callaghan.

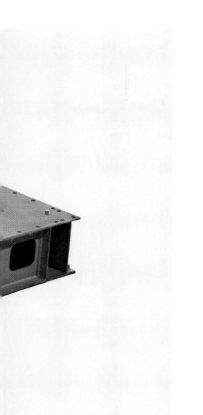

5.

THE SIXTIES

Small engines grow into big business

There was a strong focus during the 1960s on the development of Evendale's large engines—particularly the high bypass turbofan—to meet commercial, military, and marine and industrial requirements. Lynn's engine business had been steadily increasing as well.

In the early 1960s, the T64 was drawing impatient stares from management because, although it had been originally conceived by the Navy and GE as a long term development program, it still had no applications. Ed Woll took the challenge and entered the T64 in a Navy competition for a heavy helicopter. Sikorsky and Boeing Vertol were the airframe competitors. The original studies called for power from three Avco Lycoming T55s. Woll and his Lynn engine team believed the helicopter would perform even better with two T64s. Sikorsky proposed a twin-T64-powered helicopter and won the Navy CH-53 contract. The helicopter/engine requirement provided a production base for the T64—and a long history of trouble-free CH-53 operational service.

1.

1. Len Heurlin.
2. T64 production.

T64-powered aircraft:
3. Sikorsky CH-53 helicopter;
4. deHavilland DHC-5 Buffalo transport;
5. Fiat (Aeritalia) G.222 transport;
6. Shin Meiwa PS-1 flying boat;
7. Chance Vought XC-142 VTOL research transport.

3.

2.

From that base the T64 became the choice for a wide and unusual variety of helicopters and aircraft. The GE T64 team under the leadership of Len Heurlin worked closely with deHavilland of Canada. Their short takeoff turboprop, the Buffalo, was soon powered by two T64s. The Buffalo went into service with Canada's air force and into commercial service in other nations. Although the Buffalo was unofficially selected by the U.S. Army, the mission it was to perform for that service was assumed by the Air Force and the airplane was never operational with the U.S. military. The Japanese Navy selected the T64 for both its PS-1 flying boat and P2J patrol aircraft. The T64, replacing two RR Darts, was chosen by Fiat of Italy for its G.222 transport.

In the mid-1960s the Army held a major competition for a new advanced helicopter. The mission established for the chopper required a radical design since it would be called on to perform high speed dashes to the target, to be extremely maneuverable in tight, close-to-the-ground situations, and also to carry weapons for enemy strikes. Lockheed and GE designers worked together on airframe/engine integration. The result was the AH-56—an agile helicopter equipped with short wings. In January, 1968, the U.S. ordered 375 AH-56s and the T64 was well on its way. But the combat conditions of Southeast Asia and defense budget constraints dictated a shift in weapons system requirements. Before the development program had been completed, the AH-56 was terminated.

To meet the diverse applications of the combined turboshaft/turboprop T64, the basic engine grew from its original 2,600-2,800 horsepower level to the 5,000 horsepower class. On helicopters, the T64 operates as a turboshaft and on conventional aircraft such as the Buffalo, PS-1, P2J and G.222 the engine shaft turns the propeller's reduction gear. The T64 marked several technology advances: the first titanium compressor, designed to resist salt water corrosion in Navy service; the first use of high temperature coating of the turbine for corrosion resistance; and the first time a gas turbine engine was designed to operate vertically. The T64 continues to have the lowest specific fuel consumption of any turboshaft engine in helicopter service.

4.

5.

6.

7.

THE SIXTIES

T58/T64 production at Lynn

At Lynn the turboprop and turboshaft T58 and T64 engines were providing the manufacturing "bread and butter"—the production base. Both engines were selected for an array of military and civil helicopters, VTOL and STOL (short takeoff and landing) aircraft.

1. *Hughes XV-9A hot cycle research vehicle (T64).*
2. *Kaman SH-2 helicopter (T58).*
3. *Kawasaki P2J ASW aircraft (T64).*
4. *Boeing Vertol CH-46 helicopter (T58).*
5. *Sikorsky VH-3 Presidential helicopter (T58).*
6. *Sikorsky S-62 helicopter (T58).*
7. *Boeing Vertol V-107 helicopter (T58).*
8. *Bell X-22A tri-service VTOL research vehicle (T58).*

3.

1.

4.

2.

5.

6.

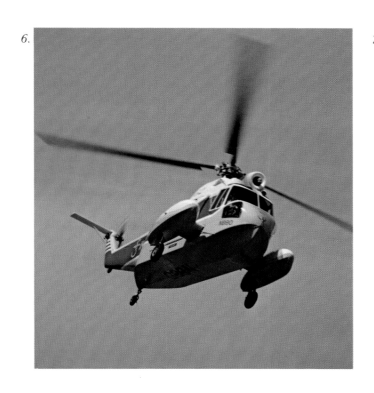

7.

8.

THE SIXTIES

J85 achieves new life

The T58 and T64 became production programs during the 1960s, but it was the J85 that emerged as the star of the Lynn show during those ten years. The J85 entered the decade of the 1970s as the Aircraft Engine Group's mass production leader, bidding for the J79's longevity record.

In early 1962, Ed Woll and his engineering team elected to start a growth program for the engine that had begun life as a non-afterburning decoy missile turbojet producing 2,950 pounds of thrust. Names that by now have become familiar ones in GE jet engine leadership were responsible for the nearly 70 percent increase in the J85's thrust output. Under Woll's direction, Art Adamson and Frank Lenherr began the original growth studies and Brian Rowe, Lee Fischer and Paul Setze and the Lynn engineering staff produced the design of what would become the J85-21 in its production version. The first step in the march toward a goal of 5,000 pounds thrust began with experimental tests in late 1962. One year later an entirely new, larger compressor was on test as part of the J85 growth program.

Northrop's original J85-powered F-5 was being produced in quantity, mostly for use as an air defense fighter in the American Military Assistance Program (MAP). Northrop, too, had been looking at a higher performance version of the F-5 for the U.S. to offer under the Foreign Military Sales (FMS) program that provided allied nations with defense equipment. GE wanted to flight test the new, higher thrust J85. The Air Force agreed to the proposal. An F-5A (the basic F-5) was bailed by the USAF to the company and Virgil Weaver's group at GE's Flight Test Center was again in the airframe modification business. The GE team at Edwards Air Force Base manufactured new engine bays for the airplane, extended the wings by about six inches and, in cooperation with Northrop's aerodynamicists, designed entirely new engine inlet ducts for the bailed F-5. Because the J85-21 engine was the radical feature of this one-of-a-kind airplane, the prototype demonstrator was designated the F-5-21.

John Fritz, then GE's chief of flight test, was to take the new "hot" little airplane aloft for the first time. The date scheduled was March 28, 1969. The time was 6 a.m. As the first flight of the advanced prototype airplane approached, the parallels between the J85 and its bigger brother, the J79, became evident. The J79 had first flown nearly 14 years before at this same site in an airplane modified by GE's Flight Test personnel. The J85 and the J79 evidenced typical characteristics of GE turbojet design. And each engine was to go on to become a high point program that provided the production base for GE's two main aircraft engine facilities, Lynn and Evendale.

Just as it had almost 14 years before when Roy Pryor readied the XF4D for the first J79 flight, came the desert dawn on the scheduled F-5-21 flight day—and the airplane was not ready. Despite the frenzied efforts of the Flight Test crew, it was still up on jacks in the hangar that morning. But Weaver and company had committed to March 28. They were determined to achieve it. The crew worked feverishly all day and by 3 p.m., John Fritz, in his orange flight suit, climbed into the compact cockpit, shut the canopy and took the F-5-21 for its first high speed taxi run. The expected small problems surfaced and nearly two hours were spent fixing them. Finally, not unlike that day nearly 14 years before when the J79 had powered an aircraft for the first time, the sun had all but disappeared behind the mountains when Fritz lifted the advanced J85-powered prototype into the desert sky for the first time. The flight lasted 40 minutes and when Fritz landed he signaled the traditional "thumbs up" that meant success. A new phase of J85 development and production had been launched that late March evening in 1969 in the California desert.

1. *Paul Setze.*
2. *J85-21 afterburning turbojet.*
3. *GE test pilot John Fritz and Northrop F-5-21 fighter (J85-21).*

1.

2.

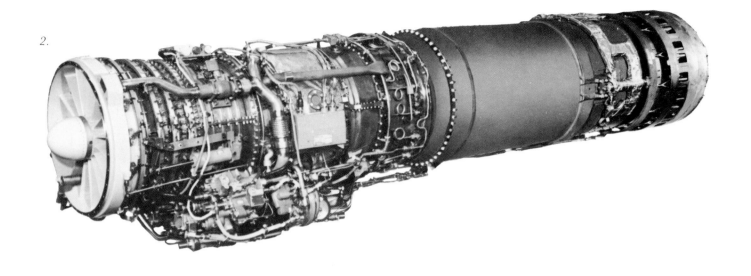

3.

THE SIXTIES

Production of J85s at Lynn began with Larry Callahan. It continued under Lou Tomasetti and the legendary Ken Bush, reaching peak production in the 1970s. In November, 1970, the U.S. government announced that the J85-powered F-5E Tiger II was to become the new International Fighter that would be offered under the FMS program for use as a defense fighter by nations allied with the United States. By 1979, nearly 2,000 of the F-5 family, including more than 1,000 F-5Es, were in service with the air arms of 26 nations around the world. The J85 logs nearly three million flight hours per year in various versions of the F-5. General Electric, according to F-5 production projections, is expected to ultimately build J85s well into the 1980s, producing more than 4,000 of an engine originally designed in 1955.

1.

2.

3.

4.

5.

1. USAF Thunderbirds flying Northrop
   T-38 Talons (J85).
2. J85-powered SAAB 105XT.
3. Rockwell T-2C trainer (J85).
4. Neumann and Northrop's Thomas
   Jones reflect on F-5/J85 program.
5. Cessna A-37 attack aircraft (J85).
6. Lockheed XV-4B VTOL research
   aircraft (J85).
7. Fiat G.91Y fighter (J85).
8. Teledyne Ryan MQM-34D MOD II
   Firebee drone (J85).

6.

7.

8.

175

THE SIXTIES

J85 spawns bizjet engines

In the early 1960s the high thrust-to-weight ratio of the non-afterburning J85 made it an attractive powerplant for the business—or executive—jets that were beginning to emerge from the drawing boards. The first study of a dry J85, later designated CJ610, was in conjunction with the famed Bill Lear, whose airframe evolved from a Swiss fighter airplane design. Two CJ610s became the powerplants for the Learjet, including a number of the subsequent models produced by Gates Learjet when that company was formed later in the 1960s. The engine was also selected to power the Aero Commander, the airplane program later purchased by Rockwell; and in the 1970s the CJ610-powered Westwind, derived from the original Aero Commander, was being produced by Israel Aircraft Industries. The engine was chosen to power the German HFB Hansa Jet, a unique forward-swept-wing business jet.

Using the basic aerodynamics of the CJ805-23 aft turbofan, GE developed an aft fan version of the J85, called the CF700. The higher thrust and increased fuel efficiency of the engine made it ideal for the French Dassault Falcon twin jet marketed worldwide by both Dassault and Pan American. Moreover, the CF700 was selected to power Rockwell's Sabre 75 version of their Sabreliner.

GE's business jet activities provided extended commercial experience for a number of Group engineers, including Brian Rowe, Fred Garry, Jim Krebs and Ted Stirgwolt. Through the 1970s, Art Adinolfi headed the company's business jet engine programs.

1.

2.

3.

4.

5.

6.

7.

8.

1. *Art Adinolfi.*
2. *Learjet (CJ610).*
3. *Westwind (CJ610).*
4. *Hansa Jet (CJ610).*
5. *CJ610 turbojet.*
6. *CF700 turbofan.*
7. *Fan Jet Falcon (CF700).*
8. *Sabre 75A (CF700).*

THE SIXTIES

Foundations laid for the 1970s...and beyond

Three other engine programs that would go on to become major segments of the Aircraft Engine Group's business in the 1970s saw their genesis at Lynn in the late 1960s.

Using GE's TF39 high bypass turbofan technology and the T64 engine core, the company in 1967-68 established design specifications for an advanced 9,000 pound thrust class engine designated the TF34. Originally selected by the Navy to power a new antisubmarine aircraft, the TF34 would become the powerplant for the U.S. Air Force's first line attack aircraft of the 1970s.

In 1967, the company began design studies on a small turboshaft engine, the GE12. The demonstrator engine, designed to produce 1,500 horsepower, achieve 20-30 percent improvement in specific fuel consumption and a 40 percent weight reduction compared to then-current engines, was intended to meet military helicopter requirements of the next decade. The GE12 was the demonstration program for GE's T700 turboshaft, selected to power three—two U.S. Army and one U.S. Navy—helicopters of the 1970s.

Building on the technology of the GE1—this time the preliminary design was a new, powerful jet engine for the next generation of lightweight fighters—the GE15 was conceived in 1967. The GE15 would become the F404, powerplant for the U.S. Navy and Marine Corps first-line fighter and attack aircraft of the 1980s and 1990s.

The initial years of the 1960s had been bleak ones. The termination of several key programs, including the U.S. SST and the B-70 bomber, plus the decision to turn away from the first 747 design, had created crises for GE's jet engine business. But these disappointments had been more than compensated for by the conception of the GE1 building block, and the resultant success of the TF39, CF6 and LM2500, and the establishment of a host of new development programs for the future. The latter-'60s growth in commercial and military aviation, particularly the emergence of high bypass turbofans, and in marine and industrial use had been recognized by the company in 1968 when it made its jet engine organization one of 10 major segments of General Electric's business structure.

General Electric entered the decade of the 1970s as well positioned in the aircraft turbine business as ever before in the history of the company.

1.

2.

3.

1. GE15 engine mockup.
2. GE12 engine mockup.
3. TF34 turbofan (front) with TF39 turbofan.
4. Northrop F-5E powered by two J85s.

4.

The Seventies...decade of achievement

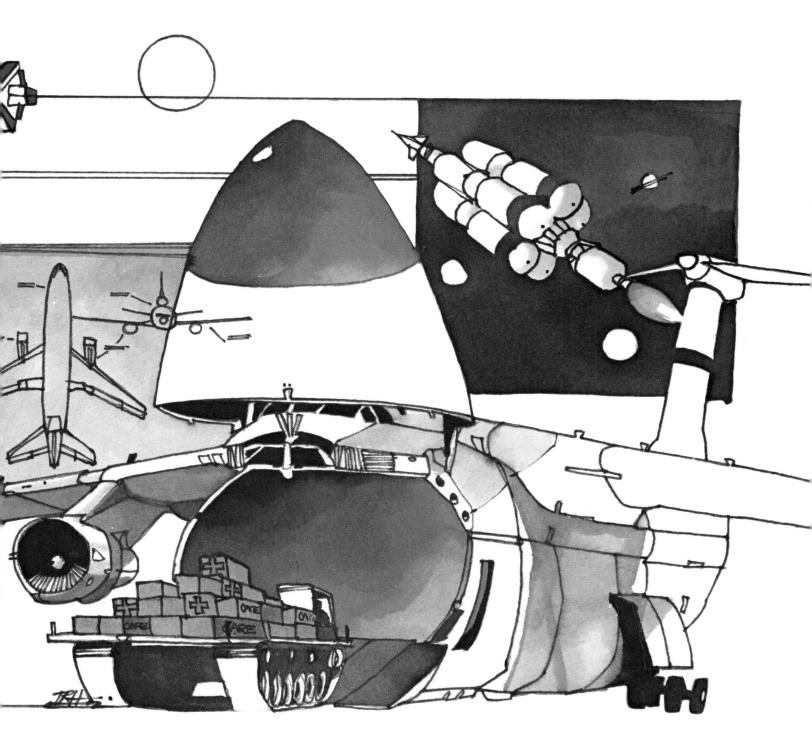

THE SEVENTIES

The ten years ending in 1969 were a decade of growth for General Electric's aircraft gas turbine business. It had become a mature, well-rounded—and significant—segment within the structure of the total company, and it was now an integral element of GE's overall growth potential for the future.

The 1970s would be a decade marked by achievement. The Aircraft Engine Group would demonstrate its ability to accomplish the commitments made in the '60s—commitments to civil aviation, to U.S. and allied defense, and to the expanding marine and industrial users of GE gas turbine engines.

By 1970 Gerhard Neumann had been a factor in GE's aircraft gas turbine business for more than 20 years, and since 1961 he had been its chief executive—and driving force. Under his leadership, the division (which became the Group in 1968) had been reshaped. It had overcome the growing pains associated with its first step into civil aviation and was on its way toward a solid position in world airline business. As the decade of the '70s dawned, nine major GE engine programs were under way.

Neumann's management and technical leadership had solidly permeated GE's aircraft engine business.

The roots of Gerhard Neumann's technical and management philosophies reach back to his youth in Germany. Lindbergh's 1927 solo flight across the Atlantic had a strong influence on the youngster. So much so that, unbeknownst to his parents and, of course, without their permission, that year he took his first airplane ride—a 15 minute flight with a barnstorming pilot operating from a grass-covered field near Neumann's hometown of Frankfurt an der Oder. ''At that moment,'' Neumann said, ''I was totally impressed—and dedicated to aviation.''

That spirit of dedication evoked in the young German student in 1927—and the educational course he chose thereafter—would have a significant impact on General Electric's aviation business in the 1960s and 1970s. Former University of California engineering school dean Mike O'Brien observed in 1975, ''The type of education Gerhard Neumann received...had a lot to do with the success of GE's aircraft engine business.''

1.

Neumann's fascination with aviation continued during his years at the "gymnasium" (comparable to the U.S. high school), and he decided to become an engineer. This time with his father's permission and encouragement, Neumann began the lengthy process required to obtain an engineering degree. The European system of the time demanded that an engineering candidate serve a minimum of three years as an apprentice mechanic in a machine shop. Neumann spent the years from 1933 to 1936 under the tutelage of a "master" qualified to train engineering degree candidates who insisted, as Neumann later put it, that his students "get black fingernails, get involved in the work, clean parts and handle them…learn welding…do everything in the machine shop…." This "hands on" training in the shop was combined with the study of mechanical theory—a curriculum that eventually enabled the young apprentice to enter the famous engineering school at Mittweida, which produced some of Germany's top aeronautical and mechanical engineers. Mike O'Brien explained, "…the Mittweida approach was to tackle an engineering problem that demanded study and understanding of the various fundamental areas of engineering. Later this type of training enabled Gerhard Neumann to be an auto mechanic, an assembler of a giant jigsaw puzzle [a Japanese Zero put together by Neumann during his

service with General Claire Chennault's Flying Tigers in China during World War II], and a GE engineer who would look at the drawings of a new engine and immediately spot the weak points. This training also led to an uncanny interest in and appreciation of product maintenance."

Neumann's training shaped the entire Aircraft Engine Group's philosophy of doing business. The "hands on" technique was required for managers and engineers. "Walking the shop" to observe what was happening and to discuss mutual objectives was common—even during the second and third shifts. "Do it right the first time" became a basic credo. Perhaps of greatest significance to GE's ability to achieve its present position in civil aviation was the Neumann-inspired dedication to continued maintenance of the group's products in operational service, a lesson well-learned from GE engine experience during the Vietnam conflict.

So intense was the business and technological drive exerted by GE's Aircraft Engine Group that during a major aircraft engine competition a large photograph of Gerhard Neumann was posted in one competitor's plant with a caption that read, "THIS MAN WANTS YOUR JOB!"

GE's long-time Aircraft Engine Group legal counsel, Jim Sack, observed, "Gerhard Neumann has an uncanny sense of the do-able."

1. GE maintenance of gas turbines in service.
2. Japanese Zero reconstructed by Gerhard Neumann.
3. Jim Sack.

2.

3.

Gas turbine technology advancement: a hallmark

From the early 1950s, when Jim LaPierre first created a separate organization in the Aircraft Gas Turbine division exclusively for the study and development of advanced concepts in engines, materials and processes, and energy sources, looking to the future was a hallmark of GE's jet engine progress. "Anticipate the requirements of the business—be ready when the need surfaces" best summarizes that philosophy. The list of men responsible for the leadership of this technology advancement reads like a "Who's Who" of GE's aircraft engine business: Sam Puffer, Dave Cochran, John Blanton, Don Berkey, Jim Krebs, Fred MacFee, Fred Garry, Ed Woll, Brian Rowe, Morris Zipkin, to name a few.

From seeds planted early in the 1960s sprang the GE engines, the materials, the processes—the advances—of the latter years of the '60s and the 1970s. The "building block" concept, which provided an economical approach to the problem of proliferating customer requirements, matured during this time.

From the labs had come a number of other innovations: techniques for achieving engine operating temperatures previously considered impossible; high bypass turbofans that increased engine thrust by a factor of three over then current powerplants; designs that enabled turbine engines to operate more efficiently than their predecessors; and the invention of new alloys to meet the unique demands of high performance jet engine operation.

Out of GE's engine research lab had come a complete family of alloys, the René series of nickel-based metals in combination with chrome, molybdenum, cobalt, aluminum and titanium. In the '60s, under the leadership of Lou Jahnke, the Evendale materials lab had developed René "on order" to meet the high strength, high temperature requirements that engine designers forecast for the '70s. Derivatives of René, first developed for the J79 engine, were used on the GE4, TF39, CF6, F101, F404 and T700.

1.

2.

The Advanced Engineering and Technology Programs department of the 1970s, under the management of Morris Zipkin, applied considerable effort to easing the environmental impact of engine operation through its work on noise suppression and exhaust emission control. GE had been the first U.S. engine maker to actively tackle the problem of jet engine noise when it designed the so-called "daisy" sound suppressor (it made the rear of the engine look like a perfectly formed flower) for the CJ805 turbojet on the Convair 880. This program had provided the company with extensive knowledge about the sound phenomena of both engine exhaust and compressor operation. This experience led to the development of sound suppression techniques for all aspects of the engine, and even included altering engine aerodynamics to reduce the roar of the jet's exhaust. One of the great benefits of the high bypass turbofan was its low exhaust sound. The turbofan-powered widebody jetliners of the '70s enabled the airlines to become better community neighbors—and set sound standards against which other jets were measured. A GE development and demonstration program in the '70s was the company's contribution to NASA's "quiet engine" studies.

4.

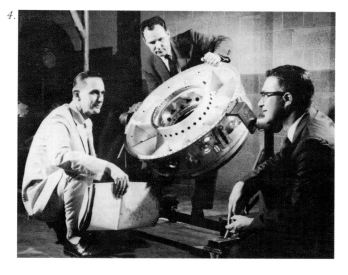

3.

5.

1. Morris Zipkin with a NASA "quiet engine" fan frame.
2. Lou Jahnke.
3. CJ805 "daisy" sound suppressor on Convair 880.
4. René 41 compressor rear frame for J79 with Lou Jahnke, Larry Wilbers, and Ralph Patsfall.
5. Advanced development facilities at Evendale.

THE SEVENTIES

Jet aircraft of the early days could be quickly identified and easily tracked by their trail of black exhaust gases, particularly at takeoff. GE's engine lab originally tackled that problem in the 1960s by developing a modified and improved combustion system for the J79. This early work produced the "smokeless" engines—both military and civil—of the 1970s.

Not satisfied that all of the frontiers of gas turbine technology had been conquered, General Electric's aircraft engine laboratory in the 1970s focused on the complexities of matching high performance powerplants with equally high performance airframes to achieve optimum system efficiency. Out of the lab came applications for composite materials to reduce engine structure weight and extend parts life in operation. The new technology of microprocessors and silicon chips is enabling GE engine controls to become digital electronic systems. As engines grew in both size and power, more efficient aerodynamics were applied to compressor, turbine and fan blades.

Among the leaders in advancing GE technology and manufacturing expertise were Bill Cornell, Ralph Patsfall, and Ken Stalker. And, although attention in the 1960s had been focused on the demonstration and development of increasingly larger engines such as the TF39, CF6, GE4 and LM2500, particular concentration in the 1970s was given to the development of smaller, more efficient engines. Demonstrator engines of the 1970s such as the GE25, 26 and 27 could be GE's production, operational engines of the 1980s. The GE26 is the smallest aircraft gas turbine ever designed by GE and was conceived as an expendable powerplant.

The Aircraft Engine Group's technical achievements were recognized by General Electric in the 1970s when four distinguished jet engine veterans were honored with the Charles P. Steinmetz award. The Group's honorees were Joe Alford, Clarence Danforth, Marty Hemsworth and Art Adamson. The biennial Steinmetz award, started in 1973, honors people whose technical contributions have helped shape both a better company and a better society.

1.

2.

3.

4.

1. Bill Cornell.
2. Ralph Patsfall.
3. Ken Stalker.
4. "Smokeless" TF39s (left) on C-5A.
5. Engine components made of composites.

THE SEVENTIES

A defeat produces increased determination

In the late 1960s the U.S. Department of Defense had established requirements for the next generation of Air Force and Navy air combat fighters. DoD, continuing to seek commonality of military weapons systems, determined that the engines for these two aircraft should be based on an identical core (compressor, combustor and turbine)—but recognized that added components such as fan and afterburning concepts would be unique to either USAF or USN requirements. The Navy had already chosen the Grumman F-14 Tomcat to provide the fleet's long range air defense in the 1970s and 1980s. The Pratt & Whitney TF30 (then powering the TFX/F-111) was selected for the initial F-14s, but the intent was that ultimately the F-14 would be reengined with the newer, more powerful design emanating from the joint USAF/USN development program. McDonnell Douglas, in a competition with Grumman, was selected to develop the USAF fighter, the F-15 Eagle.

GE fully recognized that the new engine could be its next J79. (J79-powered F-4s had established a commonality pattern and were by then in operational service with the USAF, USN, and USMC, plus a number of allied nations.) A team of GE engineers, under the direction of Ed Woll and Jim Worsham and including Bob Hawkins, Dick Taylor and George Ward, with Tom Harmon providing liaison with Wright Field, began a determined effort to design an engine combination to meet both Air Force and Navy requirements. Building on the GE1 core engine base, the team evolved the GE9 and GE1/10 demonstrator engines designed to meet Air Force requirements for the next generation bomber, then called AMSA (Advanced Manned Strategic Aircraft). This technology provided a base for a new family of engines, including the GE proposal for the F-15 and F-14.

1.

The events surrounding the preparation of the proposal and the oral presentations at Wright Field were reminiscent of the TF39/C-5 effort. But the outcome was not. In February, 1970, Pratt & Whitney was selected to produce the F100 engine for the F-15 and the F401 for the F-14.

Jim Worsham, later analyzing the competition, observed, "We never convinced the Air Force that GE knew as much as the competitor about inlet/fan compatibility."

The F100-powered F-15 entered USAF operational service in the mid-1970s. The Navy's F-14, however, continued to be powered by the original TF30 as late as 1979. After extensive Navy, Defense Department and Congressional studies, the F401 engine development program was terminated in the middle years of the '70s.

GE's aircraft engine management and technology team vowed that inability to respond to customer perceptions would never again be a factor; and with added determination attacked the challenge of the AMSA engine competition.

1. *F100 demonstrator engine (F400 for USN had same core engine).*

2. *Jim Worsham with GE1/10 (right) mockup, predecessor to GE F100/F400 demonstrator for F-15/F-14 competition.*

2.

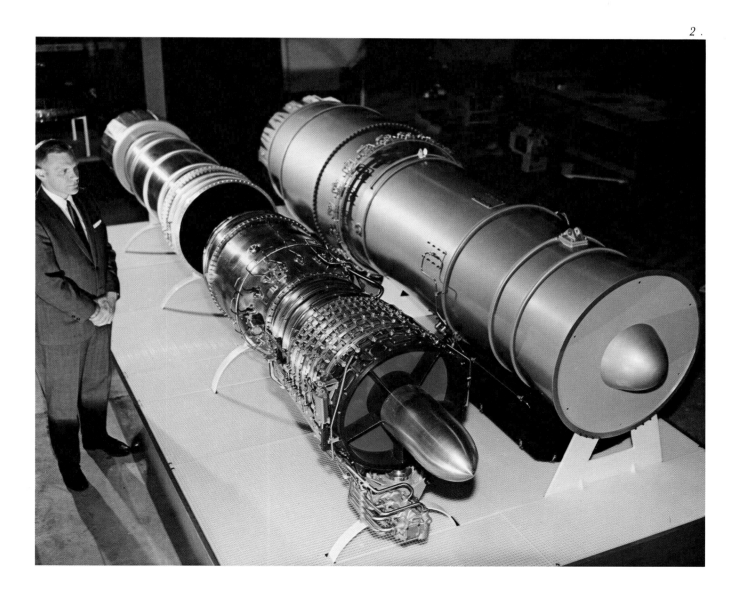

Another building block is set in place

The strategic requirement for the "next generation" U.S. long range bomber had been changed by the Defense Department and the Air Force in the 1960s. The XB-70 program had been terminated and in its place had been created the Advanced Manned Strategic Aircraft (AMSA) study. In 1967 the Air Force provided funding to GE so that the company could accelerate its own development of the GE9 as a potential powerplant for AMSA. Under Ed Woll's direction, a team including Bill Rodenbaugh, Hank Russell, Hank Schnitzer, Bill Collier and Bob Hawkins produced an engine design for a 30,000 pound thrust powerplant capable of propelling AMSA at speeds of Mach 2. During the final phase of the design effort, the loss of the F-15/F-14 engine contracts was fresh in the minds of the GE team. Airframe/engine inlet compatibility was a prime criterion. Project manager Paul Dawson assigned Dick Taylor the responsibility of working with North American Rockwell, George Ward was to work with General Dynamics, and Dawson would work with Boeing. The three airframe companies were competing for the AMSA contract.

The GE9-derived engine for AMSA drew upon technology from GE's X370 development; it utilized René alloys created in the materials laboratory; it was a turbofan with a 2.2-to-1 bypass ratio; and it was the company's first afterburning turbofan.

The deep resolve to win triggered by the unsuccessful competition earlier in the year paid off. In June, 1970, the Air Force selected GE to develop and produce the F101 engine for AMSA. North American Rockwell was later selected to build the airframe for the USAF strategic bomber of the 1970s, 1980s and beyond—the B-1.

1. Bill Rodenbaugh.
2. Paul Dawson.
3. Hank Schnitzer.
4. Bill Collier.
5. Dick Taylor.
6. George Ward.

The F101 Project was established with Jim Worsham as general manager and George Ward as B-1 program manager. The building of prototypes began and, following initial hardware testing in the early '70s and the delivery of engines to Rockwell, the sleek swept-wing, supersonic B-1 lifted off the runway at Palmdale in the California desert on December 23, 1974. After a one-hour and eighteen-minute shakedown cruise through the desert skies, the B-1 settled gently onto the Edwards Air Force Base runway. The B-1—and the F101 engine—program was proceeding as planned.

By late 1976 GE had produced 46 engines for the B-1. The engine had accumulated more than 12,000 hours of testing, including approximately 400 hours of flight test in the aircraft. The USAF/Rockwell flight test program for the B-1 had demonstrated the airplane's capabilities.

The strategic significance of the B-1 became a factor in U.S.-Soviet SALT II negotiations and, in 1977, President Jimmy Carter's administration decided to terminate the B-1 program. Some further flight testing, including engine tests, was continued to insure that the technological advances represented by the B-1/F101 were not lost.

Responding to the poor prospects in the late '70s for both civil and military engine development programs, which was caused in part by U.S. Congressional desires to curtail defense budgets in favor of other new programs, GE modified the basic F101 with a new fan and afterburning system. The F101 DFE (Derivative Fighter Engine) offered potential for a variety of fighter and attack aircraft, including two Navy aircraft—the F-14B and a reengined Vought A-7. The F101 DFE was also considered as an alternative for the USAF F-16 lightweight fighter. In addition, the F101 core became the basis for the CFM56, a civil engine that was to provide an entirely new facet to GE's aircraft engine business for the 1970s, '80s and beyond.

8.

9.

10.

11.

7. F101 afterburning turbofan with USAF plant representatives Col. P.G. Schultz and Maj. J.C. Shockley.
8., 9. & 10. Rockwell B-1 strategic aircraft.
11. F101 DFE Derivative Fighter Engine.

THE SEVENTIES

Three military programs prosper in the 1970s

The TF34 high bypass turbofan, derived in the late '60s from the TF39 and CF6, was the first of three engine programs that restored GE's position in the military engine business.

The TF34 project was aimed at a Navy antisubmarine aircraft. It was originally directed by Art Adamson and Denis Edkins and later by Bob Ingraham and Len Heurlin with strong support from Dave Gerry, Ted Stirgwolt and from George Behlmer, who provided liaison with the Navy as their antisubmarine aircraft requirements evolved. The TF34 ''mini'' high bypass engine was proposed to the Navy on January 1, 1968. For the next several months, as the competing offers were evaluated, some pessimism began to permeate the Lynn management and engineering ranks. Ed Woll received a phone call from Washington on April 1. The voice at the other end of the line said it was Navy Captain ''Red'' Kelly, calling to inform Woll that GE had won the engine competition. Even Ed Woll had been infected by a bit of pessimism—and it *was* April 1. Woll responded, ''Is this some kind of April Fool's joke?'' It wasn't. GE was to provide the TF34 for the Navy's new S-3A antisubmarine warfare aircraft. The plane would be built by Lockheed, who had won the contract following an intense competition with Grumman.

As was true of all sophisticated aircraft development programs of the 1960s and 1970s, airframe/engine matching became a prime consideration, requiring extensive coordination between Lockheed and GE as their designs evolved. Significant data were generated from a GE TF34 flight test program conducted by the company's veterans at the Edwards Flight Test Center. Well in advance of the first flight of the S-3A, the TF34 was thoroughly flight tested on a Boeing B-47 that GE leased from the Air Force.

The aircraft carrier-based S-3A entered Navy service in February, 1974; the first full squadron was sent to the Mediterranean aboard the USS John F. Kennedy in July, 1975, as scheduled.

1.

2.

1. Bob Ingraham.
2. Dave Gerry.
3. TF34 turbofan trimetric.
4. Ted Stirgwolt.
5. Lou Tomasetti.
6. Steve Chamberlin.
7. TF34 installed on Boeing B-47 flying test bed.

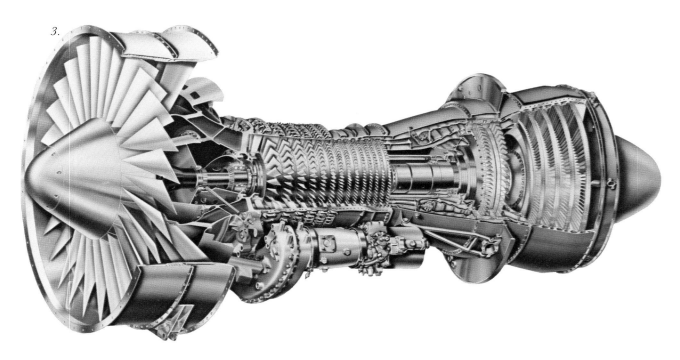

In the late 1960s the Air Force established requirements for the A-X, a new high performance, agile ground attack aircraft which would provide close air support for infantry forces.

In a departure from recent past practice, the Defense Department announced that the contract would go to the winner of a flyoff competition—in which the two finalist aircraft were to be flight tested by a USAF evaluation team. This "fly before buy" concept was designed to reduce overall costs of new weapon system acquisition. Also to control costs, DoD placed a ceiling on the cost of the total aircraft weapon system. To meet these strictures, the airframe competitors would obviously have to design around existing powerplants. This procedure contrasted sharply with the pattern of engine runoffs followed by airframe competitions that had been standard since the 1950s.

The two A-X finalists selected in December, 1970, were Northrop's A-9, designed around an Avco Lycoming YF102, and Fairchild Republic's A-10, powered by the Navy-funded and developed GE TF34. Frank Pickering, who would become the Group's engineering general manager, was in charge of TF34 engineering. Because the "fly before buy" concept was an entirely new experience for most of the DoD evaluators (many had not even begun their military careers when the last flyoff had taken place), the competition became a real horse race. Both companies built two prototypes that began flight tests in 1972 and then in the fall of that year were turned over to a joint USAF flight test team at Edwards Air Force Base. After an intensive two-month evaluation of each aircraft's capabilities, the TF34-powered A-10 was chosen in late 1972 as the USAF's new close air support aircraft.

Under the direction of project managers Lou Tomasetti and Steve Chamberlin, the GE TF34 had chalked up its second major application—this time for the Air Force. The engine was now a multiservice program. The A-10 entered operational service with the USAF in the second half of the 1970s and is expected to be a front-line operational system well into the 1980s.

4.

5.

6.

7.

THE SEVENTIES

1. TF34—power for S-3A and A-10.
2., 3. & 4. Lockheed S-3A Viking in U.S. Navy service.

5.

6.

5., 6. & 7. *Fairchild Republic A-10 Thunderbolt II in U.S. Air Force service.*

7.

THE SEVENTIES

Radical design for a GE helicopter engine

Concurrent with the evolution of the 1960s-conceived TF34, another Lynn-designed engine was following a parallel path. For this engine, however, the target was a new U.S. Army helicopter. In 1967, General Electric had been awarded an Army technology demonstrator contract for the GE12. Pratt & Whitney had been awarded a similar contract. The new engine was to be a low cost, easily maintainable 1,500 horsepower turboshaft. The requirements also included substantially improved fuel consumption, greater reliability and a significant weight reduction compared with then-current engines.

The GE12 was a radical company design. It combined both axial and centrifugal flow in the compressor. GE had not used centrifugal flow compressors since the 1940s. But memories (and data preservation) are long. The GE12 combination compressor, with an innovative design and fabrication technique, was to prove decisive. The Army, seeking minimum field maintenance and low cost, said that one criterion for evaluating the engine would be the number of parts in the engine. Intelligence reports indicated GE's competitor had an efficient 14-to-1 compressor with only seven major parts in its rotor. When GE designers finished counting the number of pieces in their compressor rotor, the total was more than 300. Back to the drawing board. The result was a unique design called the "blisk" that the manufacturing engineers, under the direction of Bill Lindsay, said they could build. Instead of each stage of the compressor consisting of many individual blades fitted into a center disk, the design/manufacturing team developed a process to machine the entire stage from a single piece of metal. The one-piece unit—blades and disk—was christened "blisk." The GE12 compressor rotor now had only nine parts.

1.

2.

196

In the final stages of the evaluation, the Army ran sand erosion tests to ascertain the reliability of the engine under field operating conditions. The GE12's centrifugal/axial compressor demonstrated a two percent efficiency increase; the competitor's had markedly deteriorated.

In March, 1972, the Army awarded GE a contract for the production version of the GE12, designated the T700. Originally begun in 1967 under Art Adamson, the GE12/T700 was the result of the technical leadership of Ed Woll and Fred Garry with contributions from such people as Jim Krebs, Pete Chipouras, Bob Turnbull and, particularly, the T700's project manager in the '70s, Bill Crawford.

Tony Rodes had brought the Army and GE together in a first-ever helicopter engine development program between that service and the company.

The initial Army helicopter application for the T700 was the UTTAS (Utility Tactical Transport Aircraft System), later designated UH-60A. Since the Army had already selected the engine, both the Sikorsky and Boeing Vertol entries in the competition were designed around the T700. Following a series of extensive flight tests in 1974-75, Sikorsky was selected to build the T700-powered UH-60A. Duane Semcken, long associated with GE turboshaft engines, continued his on-site liaison with Connecticut helicopter manufacturers. The utility helicopter entered Army operational service in the latter 1970s and is expected to continue providing ground forces support for the 1980s and 1990s.

1. Bill Crawford.
2. "Blisk" (below) and complete T700 axial-centrifugal compressor rotor.
3. Fred Garry.
4. T700 turboshaft engine.

3.

4.

THE SEVENTIES

The lessons learned from ground forces operations in Vietnam had created the requirements for another Army weapon system, the Advanced Attack Helicopter (AAH). Once again the Army's new T700 turboshaft was selected to power both entries in the final flyoff competition. Bell Helicopter and Hughes Helicopters reached the finals of the competition for the advanced, sophisticated Army chopper following a spirited effort involving most of America's prime helicopter designers. The AAH, later designated the YAH-64, utilizes a number of sophisticated electronic and aerodynamic techniques to enable the aircraft to operate in rugged terrain, using high speed and agility to outmaneuver enemy forces.

The initial flights of the T700-powered Bell and Hughes helicopters took place within two days of each other in September-October, 1975. The flyoff competition was completed in late 1977. Hughes was selected by the Army to develop the YAH-64. Bell later designed the 214ST to use two T700s in place of one T55 engine.

Historically in the U.S., gas turbine engines for helicopters have been developed by one military service and then adapted to meet requirements of one or more of the other services. The T700 was no exception. It had been developed by General Electric for the Army and powered two of their principal choppers. The U.S. Navy later established requirements for a Mark III version of the Light Airborne Multi-Purpose System helicopter, the SH-60B Seahawk. The T700 was selected to power the Navy aircraft. As the decade of the '70s concluded, the T700 was in full production for first-line military operational helicopters for service in the 1980s and beyond.

1. *T700 production at Lynn.*
2. *Ed Woll receives Klemin Award from J.F. Atkins, (president, Bell Helicopter) chairman, American Helicopter Society, 1975.*

T700-powered:
3. *Sikorsky UH-60A Black Hawk;*
4. *Hughes YAH-64 attack helicopter;*
5. *Bell 214ST helicopter;*
6. *Sikorsky SH-60B Seahawk.*

3.

4.

5.

6.

The next J79?

With only one exception, every jet aircraft Northrop had designed since the late 1940s had been built around a General Electric gas turbine engine. It was only natural for Northrop airplane designers to turn to a GE powerplant when the company in the late '60s began studying the requirements for the next generation, multi-role, air combat fighter to succeed the F-5 family. Northrop's Tom Jones and the company's product planners believed the philosophy embodied in the F-5 for the '60s and '70s—high performance, low weight, low cost, capability to perform a wide range of air defense roles—would become even more desirable. Northrop anticipated that both U.S. and international requirements existed for such an aircraft through the end of the 20th century.

The engine originally studied for the new Northrop design, designated the P-530 Cobra, was a version of the J97 derivative of the GE1. The modified J97 turbojet's initial thrust rating was 8,000 pounds. When it became apparent this power rating was too low, thrust was increased to 10,000 pounds; but, by then, the GE design team was convinced that even more advanced technology was available. The evolution that would lead to the F404 turbofan was initiated.

Under Ed Woll's direction, many of the Lynn engineers who had developed the successful J85 were involved with that evolutionary process. Having been an integral part of the J85/F-5 development,

men such as Paul Setze, Jim Krebs, Pete Chipouras, and George Rapp recognized fully the type of engine needed for the lightweight, low cost weapons system being proposed by Northrop. A "design to cost" concept, using performance and cost tradeoffs, was established.

Utilizing more than two years of studies, the Lynn team in late 1969 began design of the afterburning GE15. The engine was to produce 14,300 pounds of thrust; its core was scaled down from the F101 (B-1) engine; and its design included a unique feature: a low bypass ratio fan. The ratio of fan air bypassing the compressor to the basic compressor air flow was so low in comparison to the high bypass ratio of the TF39/CF6/TF34 that the GE15 was jokingly referred to as the "leaky turbojet." But its simplicity of concept combined with the fact that it was based on proven principles and components made it ideal for the Northrop lightweight fighter. Moreover, it fitted another requirement GE had perceived.

The U.S. Air Force engine competitions of the 1960s—for the C-5, F-15 and later the B-1— had been concentrated for the most part on large, high thrust powerplants. The only engine then in production in the 15,000-20,000 pound thrust class was the 1950s-vintage GE J79. The improved J85-21 at 5,000 pounds of thrust represented the lower end of the power scale. The United States had no engine "in the middle" under development.

1.

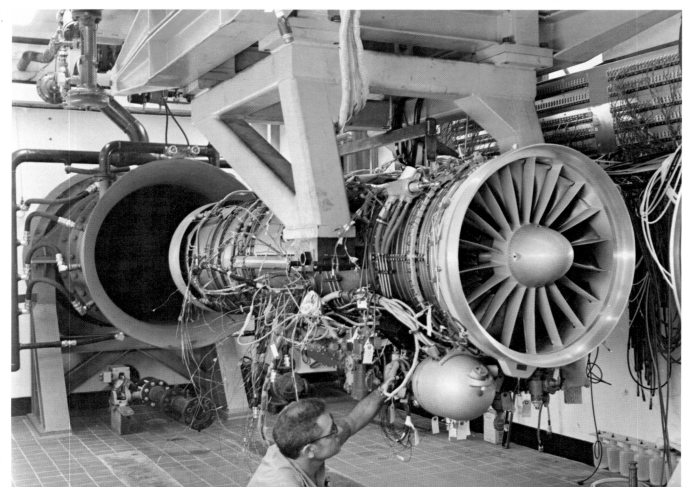

Acutely aware of what they perceived to be a void in the spectrum of America's military jet engine technology, Jack Parker and Gerhard Neumann met with then Assistant Secretary of Defense David Packard. The GE executives offered to undertake a comprehensive GE15 demonstrator program at a cost of $10 million. It would develop an engine that filled the gap between the J85 and the P&W F100: a high performance, supersonic, but relatively low cost powerplant. Although DoD had no specific aircraft requirements at the time, Packard knew well the weapons system development cycle and the long lead time required for sophisticated aircraft components—particularly engines. He asked if the Department of the Air Force could squeeze funds out of their current budget to undertake development of a GE15 demonstrator program.

Neumann met with Lt. Gen. Otto Glasser, then USAF Vice Chief of Staff, Research and Development. The two men mapped out an engine development program—complete with overall schedule and cost—on the back of the proverbial brown envelope. The USAF YJ101 engine was born. The $10 million development contract was awarded in April, 1972. When Paul Setze was named to head the YJ101 Project, Neumann gave him the brown envelope as the blueprint for his new engine program.

Meanwhile, the Air Force had begun to study the technology requirements and potential mission of a lightweight fighter as a possible complement to the larger F-15. Originally designated the lightweight fighter *technology demonstration* program, the study became a full-fledged prototype aircraft development effort in 1972. General Dynamics and Northrop were chosen from a field of four companies to design and build lightweight fighter (LWF) prototypes. No production requirements for the new airplane were established at the time, but, following the "fly before buy" concept used in the A-X competition, each company was to produce, initially test and then deliver to a joint USAF evaluation team two prototypes of the LWF. General Dynamics' airplane, powered by a single F100 (the engine selected for the F-15), was designated the YF-16; Northrop's YJ101-powered derivative of the company's P-530 Cobra was designated the YF-17. Because the Defense Department had established a "design to cost" criterion for the LWF engine, a major effort was underway at Lynn under Fred Larson and later Tony Edwards.

3.

2.

1. *YJ101 in Lynn test cell.*
2. *Northrop YF-17 (YJ101).*
3. *Jack Parker, Lt. Gen. James Stewart, and Burt Riemer at YF-17 rollout.*
4. *YF-17 model undergoing wind tunnel testing.*

The dedication to equitable business practices—design to cost, if necessary—had always been a basic Jack Parker tenet. During one earlier engine competition, Neumann informed Parker that the company might be required to accept a penalty clause for late delivery, cost overrun or performance deficiency. Parker said, "We won't accept a penalty clause without a commensurate reward." As a result of Parker's position, that contract included incentive awards as well as the penalty clause. The majority of GE's subsequent engine contracts were negotiated on that basis.

Both companies' initial LWF prototypes first flew in 1974. While they were in development, the Defense Department, recognizing that the escalating costs of large, multi-mission fighters (such as the F-14 and F-15) would severely limit the numbers that could be procured, urged that funding be budgeted for production of the new, lower cost lightweight fighter. DoD and the Congress stressed that for airplanes to meet both USAF and USN requirements for light weight fighters, they must emerge from the USAF competition—which by then had been designated the Air Combat Fighter (ACF).

General Electric produced six YJ101 flight qualified prototype engines for the two twin-engined YF-17s. That meant four engines were installed at any one time, leaving only two spares. Despite this constraint, the two YF-17s logged a total of 302 flights during the USAF accelerated flight test program between June and December, 1974. In that time, there were no in-flight shutdowns caused by engine malfunction nor was an engine ever prematurely removed from either prototype. Although the six prototype engines had originally been built in 1973-74 and developed through the 50-hour Preliminary Flight Rating Test (PFRT), three of the engines were still being used in the Northrop prototype airplane five years later. By then the two-of-a-kind aircraft and their GE prototype engines had logged more than 500 flights in demonstrations of the high performance airframe/engine combination conducted in France, England, Canada and the U.S. The twin engine prototype had made four separate North Atlantic crossings.

Veteran Northrop chief test pilot Hank Chouteau, who had personally flown the GE-powered prototypes on the great majority of their missions, characterized the YJ101s as "the most responsive, trouble-free engines I have ever been associated with."

1. F404 engine on test at Lynn.
2. F404 turbofan engine.
3. Burt Riemer.
4. Frank Pickering.
5. Pete Chipouras.

1.

2.

In January, 1975, the Air Force selected the F100-powered YF-16 for their new Air Combat Fighter. In May, 1975, the Navy chose a derivative of the YF-17 prototype. It was designated the F-18 Hornet. The F-18 was modified for aircraft carrier suitability and would replace two of the Navy and Marine Corps, first-line fighter and attack aircraft, the F-4 and A-7, in operational service in the 1980s and 1990s. In order to meet the Navy's multipurpose requirements, the GE engine, now designated the F404, was uprated to 16,000 pounds thrust and the bypass ratio increased for more efficient operation.

In late 1974, during the ACF competition, Northrop and McDonnell Douglas had agreed to a joint development and production effort on the major USAF/USN air combat fighter program. For the Air Force competition, Northrop would be prime contractor, with McDonnell Douglas as principal subcontractor. On the Navy program, the roles would be reversed. Thus, when the Navy selected the Hornet, McDonnell Douglas became prime contractor, Northrop the principal subcontractor.

Burt Riemer was named J101 (later F404) Project manager in 1972. Riemer headed a team, including Frank Pickering and Pete Chipouras, that put the first prototype engine to test and saw it fly for the first time in 1974. Riemer and his team succeeded in convincing the Navy that the F404 would provide that service with an engine that would have 30 percent lower maintenance costs than the GE J79 (in their F-4s); would require only 40 percent of the J79 maintenance manhours; would have 40 percent fewer parts than the J79; and, for approximately the same thrust class, would be only half the weight and one-third the length of the J79.

When the Navy ordered the F-18 in 1975, the Defense Department indicated a requirement for 800 of the new multirole aircraft. In early 1979, the Navy requirement was increased to more than 1,300 of the GE-powered airplane that would provide both fleet air defense and attack capabilities into the 21st century.

The first McDonnell Douglas/Northrop F-18 Hornet was rolled out and delivered to the Navy in 1978. By 1979 initial preproduction airplanes were being flight tested by the Navy at its Patuxent River, Maryland, flight test facility; the first F-18s were scheduled to enter operational service with the USN and USMC in the early 1980s.

In 1979 nine other nations, including Canada, Australia and Israel, were considering the F-18 for their future air defense. Aviation analysts foresee a worldwide requirement for as many as 3,000 of the twin engine F-18-type aircraft. The F404 could well supplant the J79 and J85 in both longevity and total production.

3.

4.

5.

THE SEVENTIES

Marine and industrial business — and product line — grows

In 1970, when Litton and the U.S. Navy selected GE's LM2500 for the new DD-963 Spruance-class destroyers, more than the USN's first gas turbine powered combat vessel was launched. The event marked the marinization of the TF39/CF6 family for an array of naval applications.

The U.S. Navy also selected the LM2500 for the PHM-1 class of hydrofoil missile boats. The LM2500 was chosen in 1972 to power the USN Patrol Frigate FFG-7; and in 1978 it became the powerplant for the Navy's DDG-47 Aegis air defense destroyer.

From its inception, the LM2500 had international connections. Fiat of Italy had been a participant in the original LM2500 design, development and test program under a joint agreement with GE's Aircraft Engine Group. The agreement included the manufacture by Fiat of certain LM2500 parts. A team of Fred Garry, Fred MacFee, Bob Miles,

Hank Schnitzer and George Hardgrove had initiated the original agreement with Fiat. The veteran Sam Levine integrated the combined GE/Fiat LM2500 effort. In 1978, as a result of the success of the LM2500 collaboration, GE's working agreement with Fiat was extended to include a co-development program for the LM500 derivative of General Electric's TF34 turbofan engine.

The internationalization of GE's marine and industrial gas turbines was further extended when the LM2500 was selected during the 1970s to power KV-72 corvettes of the Danish navy; Italian, German, Peruvian, Venezuelan, Korean and Egyptian frigates; gunboats of both the Saudi Arabian and Indonesian navies; and in 1976 the Australian navy chose the LM2500 for three FFG-class frigates. The engine was also selected by the Italian and Spanish navies for new helicopter carriers.

1. Sam Levine.
2. O.R. ''Bud'' Bonner.
3. Spruance-class destroyer (LM2500).
4. LM2500 gasline pumper.
5. PHM hydrofoil (LM2500).
6. North Sea oil drilling platform (LM2500).
7. FFG-7 patrol frigate (LM2500).
8. Italian frigate (LM2500).
9. LM500 gas generator.
10. LM5000 gas generator.

1.

2.

3.

4.

5.

6.

7.

8.

With Sam Levine nearing retirement from the company, O.R. "Bud" Bonner was named to head the Marine and Industrial Projects department in May, 1973. Bonner, as general manager of the department through the balance of the 1970s, saw the completion of the Spruance engine production program when the 120th, and final, LM2500 was delivered for the DD-963 Spruance-class destroyers. He led the expansion of the group's M&I business to include the use of the LM2500 for power generation and gas reinjection as part of a Curtiss-Wright installation on North Sea oil drilling platforms; and for natural gas and oil pipeline transmission at a number of remote drilling sites around the world.

With the conception of a more powerful member of the CF6 commercial aviation turbofan, the CF6-50, the M&I team knew they had the basis for another step in the growing portfolio of stationary powerplants. In late 1975, the company announced the development of the LM5000, an engine in the 50,000 shaft horsepower class. The first LM5000 engine went on test at Evendale in mid-1977; the first production units were shipped in 1978 to Ishikawajima Heavy Industries (IHI) in Japan for an electric power generation installation; the second units went to GEC Gas Turbines Ltd. in the United Kingdom later that same year. The LM5000 was under study in the late 1970s for use as the powerplant in several of the naval surface effects ships (SES) then in developmental planning.

By the end of the decade of the 1970s, the viability of GE's marine and industrial segment of the company's aircraft gas turbine business had been dramatically demonstrated. Not only had the LM2500 and LM5000 been selected for a wide range of land and sea propulsion applications, but in 1979 one LM2500 engine in an industrial installation had operated for 50,000 hours—nearly six years —without overhaul.

9.

10.

THE SEVENTIES

1970s: commercial aircraft engine success achieved

The decade of the '70s marked ten years of striking progress in the development and production of new engines for important defense aircraft. These years saw the entrenchment of GE's aircraft gas turbines as power for significant industrial and marine applications. But the hallmark of the 1970s in the company's heritage of seven decades of gas turbine technology was GE's signal achievement in civil aviation.

As General Electric entered the '70s, the CF6 had been chosen to power three different jetliners. As the decade came to a close, various models of the CF6 family had been selected to power eight jet transports. Moreover, two entirely new engines for commercial aviation, the CFM56 and CF34, would add applications nine and ten to transports carrying the identification, "Powered by General Electric."

By the end of the '70s, GE had commercial engines ranging from the 8,000 pound thrust CF34 up to the 58,000 pound thrust CF6-80.

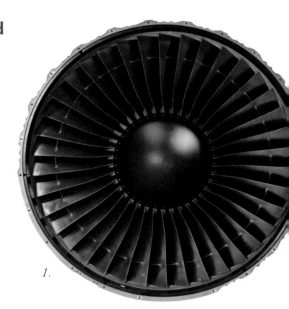

1.

2.

3.

As vice president and general manager of GE's Commercial Engine division, Ed Hood had led the company's march into the expansive years of the late 1960s and early 1970s. For GE's reconstituted civil business, the decade was underway in grand style when the first McDonnell Douglas DC-10 was rolled out in July, 1970. This unveiling was distinctive. The DC-10 was the first commercial airliner ever to roll out under its own power—the three GE CF6 engines were purring smoothly as they propelled the giant jetliner into the view of thousands of airline officials, industry guests, McDonnell Douglas and GE employees, the governor of California and the vice president of the United States. The strikingly designed widebody hove into view behind a marching contingent of kilted Scottish bagpipers and drummers who were honoring the heritage of the airframe manufacturer's two principal founders, James S. McDonnell and Donald W. Douglas. First flight of the new airplane came in August of that year, although GE had followed its tradition of flight testing the engine in advance of the airframe first flight. The CF6 had already flown on a B-52, modified by the Edwards Flight Test Center team.

The larger CF6-50 ran for the first time in September, 1970; the engine later set a new CF6 power output record when it produced 58,000 pounds of thrust. Bob Smuland, who was later to become general manager of the CF6-50 program, was an integral member of the CF6 engineering team.

Nearly 50 airlines worldwide were operating or had on order GE-powered DC-10s as the '70s ended.

4.

5.

1. *CF6 high bypass fan.*
2. *Ed Hood with DC-10 model.*
3. *CF6 married to B-52 flying test bed.*
4. *DC-10 rolls out under its own CF6 power.*
5. *DC-10 series 10 on first flight.*

The European Airbus, the A300, achieved its first sales success in 1971 when Air France ordered six of the twin CF6-powered jetliners with options for an additional ten aircraft.

Following the Air France order for A300s, Lufthansa ordered nine of the airbuses; Korean Airlines and Thai International ordered seven; Eastern Air Lines in the U.S. became the first American carrier to operate the European airplane; and by the end of the '70s, more than 20 airlines were either operating the A300 or had ordered it for 1980s service.

But 1972 was the time when General Electric achieved a share of satisfaction after nearly six years of frustration following the 1966 decision to turn away from the original competition for the Boeing 747 powerplant. The U.S. Air Force selected GE's CF6-50 to power the Airborne Command Post version of the 747, the E-4A. The engine later achieved its second military application as the powerplant for the McDonnell Douglas KC-10A Advanced Cargo Tanker. A flight test program was run on the 747 with the larger CF6 and the result was the Boeing offering of GE power for the civil 747. Many of the world's airlines were already flying P&W-powered 747s, but engine commonality became a major factor with carriers operating CF6-powered DC-10s and A300s. The GE-powered 747 was ordered first by KLM and later in the '70s by Lufthansa, Air France, UTA, All Nippon, Alia, Air Gabon, Wardair, Pakistan, Thai International, Transamerica, Libyan, Alitalia and Philippine airlines.

A solid and responsive product support network had been established under the leadership of Harry Stonecipher, who was later to head Commercial Engine Projects, and Walt VanDuyne.

In 1972 Ed Hood became the third aircraft engine executive promoted to General Electric corporate Group management when he was named vice president and group executive of the company's International Group. Brian Rowe succeeded Hood as Commercial Engine division vice president.

The company's commercial aircraft engine business in the 1970s had grown substantially and in 1974 it was divided into two divisions: Commercial Engine

1.

2.

3.

4.

5.

6.

1. Brian Rowe.
2. Neil Burgess.
3. Bob Smuland.
4. Harry Stonecipher.
5. Walt VanDuyne.
6. Bob Gerardi.

CF6-50-powered:

7. Air France A300;
8. Eastern A300;
9. E-4A Airborne Command Post;
10. KLM 747;
11. KC-10 cargo tanker;
12. Lufthansa DC-10.

7.

8.

9.

10.

Programs, including all civil engine projects plus product support, headed by Bob Goldsmith; and the Airline Programs division, responsible for sales and liaison with airline customers, headed by Brian Rowe. Later, to centralize the product support and service functions, the company's Aviation Service Shops, under Bob Gerardi, were included in the Commercial Engine division.

GE's aircraft engine international presence had been established in the 1950s and 1960s with licensing and sales of the J79, T58, J85 and T64 engines. The burgeoning worldwide civil aviation business, however, put increasing demands on the Group's requirements for international customer support, contact and liaison. By 1974 nearly half of the Aircraft Engine Group's business was outside North America and the Aircraft Engine Overseas operation was created as an organizational component. Neil Burgess, who had most recently headed European CF6 marketing, was named its general manager (and vice president of General Electric Technical Services Co.).

11.

12.

THE SEVENTIES

Four-year expansion

In the short span of only four years (1974-1978), GE had moved boldly to further strengthen its position in world aviation by expanding the responsibilites of Fred MacFee, Lou Tomasetti, Bob Goldsmith, Jim Worsham, Neil Burgess and Bud Bonner to lead its increasingly significant aircraft engine business. These men, with Ed Woll, Brian Rowe and Jim Krebs providing technology leadership, headed a well-proven team responsible for increasing customer confidence and acceptance from domestic and international civil, military, and marine and industrial users.

1.

1. F.O. MacFee staff: (top, left to right) Neil Burgess, Ralph Medros, Jim Krebs, Bob Goldsmith, Brian Rowe, Bob Desrochers, Ray Letts, Don Lester, Jim Sack; (seated, left to right) Bud Bonner, Ed Woll, Fred MacFee, Lou Tomasetti, Jim Worsham; 1978.

2. McDonnell Douglas/Northrop F-18 Hornet (F404).

3. CF6 "prep-to-ship" area in Evendale.

THE SEVENTIES

Trans-Atlantic gas turbine technology

Much as it had anticipated requirements for a military engine in the thrust class between the J85 and F100, GE management in the late 1960s recognized the need for a commercial engine in the 20,000 pound thrust class—the so-called "ten ton" engine. SNECMA, the leading French aircraft engine manufacturer, had come to the same conclusion and designed the M56 engine.

General Electric had begun studies of an engine of about the 20,000 pound thrust size. The study engine, which was based on the GE1, was called the GE13.

In addition to a number of its own engine programs, SNECMA had working agreements with both Rolls Royce and Pratt & Whitney. Reflecting France's substantial interest in the future of its aviation industry and commercial aviation in particular (France had developed the Caravelle; the A300 was being built there; the Mirage fighter and Dassault Falcon business jet were major export products), the French government encouraged SNECMA to con-

duct a competition between the two leading U.S. manufacturers for a joint development program of a medium-sized turbofan engine.

Jack Parker and Gerhard Neumann met with SNECMA officials, including the company's president, René Ravaud. A contingent of SNECMA management and technical people came to the U.S. to view firsthand the American developments at both GE and P&W. At GE they were shown the GE13. Within six months of the initial meetings, SNECMA picked General Electric for the co-development of a new engine in the 20,000 pound thrust class, called the CFM56. Because the basic CFM56 engine was designed around the core of the F101 (the powerplant for the B-1), U.S. government export licensing was required. In 1971, following a number of negotiations at the highest levels of the French and American governments, an export license was granted; and later a jointly owned company was formed and development of the "ten-ton" engine began.

1.

3.

1. *René Ravaud and Gerhard Neumann with first CFM56 engine.*
2. *Fred MacFee.*
3. *CFM56 on test at Peebles.*
4. *Jack Hope.*
5. *Frank Lenherr.*
6. *Dick Smith.*
7. *CFM56 readied for test in France.*

Fred MacFee, along with Brien Hope and Jim Sack, were credited with working out the arrangements that led to the creation of CFM International, S.A., (GE and SNECMA each hold 50 percent ownership). Bob Goldsmith and Jean-Claude Malroux established the original memo of understanding between the two principals; Fred Garry, Ed Woll, Jim Krebs, Brien Hope, Jack Hope, Bob Widen, Frank Lenherr and Bruce Gordon were instrumental in pioneering efforts to determine the technical, production, marketing and support functions of CFM International—and the role to be played by the two parent companies. SNECMA's Jean Sollier was named chief executive of CFM International; Ravaud and Neumann each served on CFM's board of directors. Jean Bagneux was SNECMA's first program manager for the CFM56; Jack Hope was GE's.

Entering the 1980s, Malroux was chief executive of the joint company. Dick Smith was GE's CFMI program's general manager; SNECMA's Jacques Rossignol was his counterpart.

Much credit for the subsequent success of the CFM56 program is given to the original agreement that clearly established a 50-50 participation in all areas, including development and production of the engine. The first CFM56 engines were built at both GE's Evendale plant and SNECMA's Villaroche, France, facility. Ironically, the jet age made possible nearly instant communications and the frequent ''eyeball to eyeball'' sessions that GE had found so important in achieving technical objectives. Rapid trans-Atlantic jet travel spawned international aircraft engine advances.

The first CFM56 engines went on test in both France and the U.S. in 1974, meeting guaranteed thrust and specific fuel consumption goals at the outset. The engine, with a 6-to-1 bypass ratio, was initially designed to produce 24,000 pounds of thrust. During its 1970s development cycle, the thrust rating was expanded and the CFM56 now ranged from 18,000 to 27,500 pounds of thrust. In recognition of environmental concerns, two specific targets were established by the joint developers of the international engine: (1) lower fuel consumption than existing powerplants in this thrust class, and (2) measurably reduced noise and emission levels. The CFM56's fuel consumption was reduced by 15-25 percent from that of earlier generation engines. Both engine sound levels and pollutant emissions were measured in operation and registered less than any other engine in airline service in the 1970s.

4.

5.

6.

7.

THE SEVENTIES

The CFM56 was first flight tested in the U.S. on a McDonnell Douglas YC-15 and in France on a Caravelle. The YC-15 and the Boeing YC-14 (powered by two GE CF6-50 engines) competed for a USAF development program for the next generation of Air Force medium range transports, AMST (Advanced Medium STOL Transport). The CFM56 was considered a strong candidate to power the YC-15 AMST, but the program was postponed by the U.S. government in the late 1970s. The French Caravelle, of course, had been used in 1961 to demonstrate America's first turbofan engine, GE's CJ805-23.

In the late 1970s Boeing offered the CFM56 as a retrofit engine for its 707. The new engine would enable 707 operators to meet noise and emission standards established in the 1970s. Flight test engines were delivered to Boeing for the CFM56-powered 707-700 in 1979 and the first flight of the retrofitted airplane took place in late 1979.

1.

2.

General Electric, SNECMA and CFM International officials had been working closely with McDonnell Douglas management on DC-8 retrofit and in March and April, 1979, the first breakthrough came for the CFM56. In March 1979 new group executive Fred MacFee announced that United Airlines, Flying Tiger Line and Delta Air Lines had selected the engine for retrofit of more than 50 DC-8-60 series aircraft. Later in 1979 Capitol, Cargolux and Spantax ordered the CFM56 for their DC-8 transport reengining.

In an April 30, 1979 article about the DC-8 reengining program, *Aviation Week & Space Technology* magazine said, ''The inherent operating economics of the DC-8 Series 60 aircraft and the increasing costs for aircraft replacement make the stretched DC-8s attractive reengining candidates.'' The magazine continued, ''The CFM56 engines will reduce fuel consumption and enable the DC-8s to meet new federal U.S. noise requirements.'' In the article, a Flying Tiger Line senior vice president was quoted as saying, ''...the lower noise level of the CFM56 when compared to the competitive engine was an influential factor in the...selection of the General Electric/SNECMA powerplant.'' The Flying Tiger executive went on to say in *Aviation Week*, ''Additionally, the CFM56 engines give us approximately 3 percent more range on the Series 60 aircraft.''

Clearly, the viability of the CFM56 engine for jetliners of the 1980s and beyond had been established in the late 1970s.

1. *CFM56 on right nacelle of Caravelle.*
2. *McDonnell Douglas YC-15 with CFM56 (right).*
3. *CFM56 testing with Boeing 707 nacelle at Peebles.*
4. *CFM56/707 aerodynamic testing.*
5. *McDonnell Douglas DC-8 series 60 model with CFM56 engines.*

4.

3.

5.

215

Three new applications call for CF6 power

The final year of the decade of the 1970s was an eventful time for General Electric's aircraft gas turbine business. Not only had the CFM56 logged its first sales but three major new jetliners that would serve passengers through the end of the 20th-century had been ordered or offered with members of the CF6 family.

In 1978 Boeing startled the world aviation industry with the announcement of its intent to add two new airplanes, the 757 and 767, to its highly successful 700 series of jetliners (707, 727, 737, 747). The new Boeing airplanes were being developed to take advantage of the advanced engine technology embodied in the high bypass turbofan, the experience gained from initial widebody jetliner service and ac-

ceptance, and the obvious potential of high speed, economical air service as the accepted medium and long distance mass transportation of the future. The Boeing 757 is a two engine standard body jet transport for short-to-medium routes. The 767 is a larger widebody twin engine transport designed for medium range service.

The 767 was launched in mid-1978 with a United Airlines order. The airline had selected P&W JT9 engines. The airplane had been offered with GE's CF6-6, but United had introduced transcontinental range requirements late in the competition and the GE engine did not meet these thrust requirements. Following the United order GE immediately began a design effort to upgrade their basic engine's

1.

2.

specifications, using new technology to increase thrust and significantly lower fuel consumption and weight. The result was the CF6-80, producing between 48,000 and 58,000 pounds of thrust. The first engine ran successfully on test in October 1979.

In late 1978 American Airlines and Delta Air Lines ordered 50 of the GE-powered Boeing 767s.

Although the 757 had been launched in 1978 with orders from Eastern Air Lines and British Airways for a Rolls Royce RB211-powered version, the 757 was also being offered with the GE CF6-32 high bypass turbofan. This 36,500 pound thrust engine, derived from the CF6-6 but utilizing a smaller diameter fan, was being developed by GE in cooperation with Alfa Romeo or Italy, SNECMA of France and Volvo Flygmotor of Sweden.

Airbus Industrie in late 1978 announced a new model of the airbus family, the A310, an airplane in competition with the Boeing 767. In early 1979, Lufthansa and KLM announced an $800 million order for 35 of the new CF6-80-powered twinjets. Swissair ordered a quantity of the JT9-powered A310.

At the lower end of the power scale, the commercial derivative of GE's military TF34, the CF34, was selected in the late 1970s as the powerplant for a new, twin engine jet transport being developed by Canadair of Canada. Named the Challenger E, the airplane was designed as both a higher capacity, longer range business aircraft than then-current executive jets as well as a jet transport for airlines serving lower density routes.

By the end of the decade of the '70s, more than 60 airlines were operating or had ordered General Electric-powered civil transports. Seven different GE high bypass turbofan engines were in development or production to power at least ten separate aircraft. General Electric had achieved a firm presence as a designer, developer and producer of aircraft engines for commercial as well as military aviation.

5.

3.

6.

4.

1. CF6-80 turbofan engine mockup.
2. CF6-32 on test at SNECMA.
3. Boeing 767 (CF6-80).
4. Airbus Industrie A310 (CF6-80).
5. CF34 turbofan engine.
6. Canadair Challenger E (CF34).

THE SEVENTIES

A decade—and an era—come to an end, a new era emerges

By the end of 1979, Jack Parker had been associated, directly and indirectly, with the evolution of General Electric's aircraft gas turbine progress for nearly thirty years, Gerhard Neumann for more than thirty years. The Parker/Neumann team had left an indelible mark on GE, on jet engines, and on world aviation.

In late 1977 Gerhard Neumann for health reasons turned over the reins of the business he had led for 17 years. Fred O. MacFee, Jr., an executive who had been an integral part of the technology advances, of the strategic business planning and of the marketing and product expansion and achievements of the '50s, '60s and '70s, on April 1, 1978, was named vice president and group executive of GE's Aircraft Engine Group. The announcement was made by Ed Hood, then GE's corporate sector executive whose responsibility included the company's aircraft engine business as well as other high technology segments of the company's business.

For the balance of 1978 and 1979 Neumann served as a corporate vice president assigned to Jack Parker for special projects to "work with General Electric management and customers in order to further Aircraft Engine Group objectives." He retired from the company December 31, 1979.

In 1979 Gerhard Neumann said, "My time with General Electric was the most satisfying any person could ever have in any life."

1. 2. 3.

1. Jack S. Parker.
2. Gerhard Neumann.
3. Fred O. MacFee, Jr.
4. Edward E. Hood, Jr.
5. Brian H. Rowe and Aircraft Engine Group staff.

4.

In September, 1979, the company announced that Edward E. Hood, Jr., was elected a vice chairman and, with the retirement from the company of Jack Parker on December 31, 1979, would become a member of General Electric's board of directors.

On October 1, 1979 the transition from the Parker/Neumann/MacFee era of General Electric's progress in aircraft gas turbine technology was completed. As the final year of the decade came to a close, Reginald H. Jones, GE's chairman of the board and chief executive officer, announced that Brian H. Rowe, who had joined the company in 1957, was named a corporate senior vice president and group executive of the Aircraft Engine Group. Fred MacFee continued as a company vice president and consultant to Rowe until his retirement in January, 1980.

Rowe had served his GE "apprenticeship" on lift fan engines, was a part of the team that created the GE1 building block concept, later headed engineering for the CF700 turbofan and advanced J85, and was engineering manager at Lynn for the Small Aircraft Engine department. In 1967 Rowe became general manager of the CF6 program and in 1972 was named vice president and general manager of the Commercial Engine division. When Ed Woll retired from the company in 1979, Rowe succeeded him as the Group's vice president of engineering. The Woll/Rowe team's contributions to engine technology advancement had served the company well.

The team that Rowe headed as the company entered its eighth decade of aircraft turbine work was made up of men who had also played a prominent role in GE's advancement during the '50s, '60s, and '70s: Jim Worsham was named vice president and general manager of Commercial Engine operations; Jim Krebs headed Military Engine operations as vice president and general manager.

Reporting to Worsham and Krebs in company officer-level positions were: Neil Burgess, Airlines Program division, and Harry Stonecipher, Commercial Engine Projects division; Bill Crawford, Military Engine Projects division, and Bud Bonner, Marine and Industrial Engine Projects division.

Frank Pickering headed Group Engineering; Ray Letts was Group Manufacturing vice president; and Ralph Medros headed the Group Product Quality operation. Completing the Group staff were Jim Sack, Legal Counsel; Don Lester, Organization and Manpower; Bob Desrochers, Finance and Management Support; and Jim Kramer, Strategic Planning and Development.

In a smooth transition, as a new era emerged, General Electric leadership had evolved—as aircraft gas turbine technology evolved—through seven decades of progress.

5.

"The roads you travel so briskly lead out of dim antiquity, and you study the past chiefly because of its bearing on the living present and its promise for the future."

Lieutenant General James G. Harbord,
KCMG, DSM, LLD, U.S. Army (Ret.)
(1866-1947)

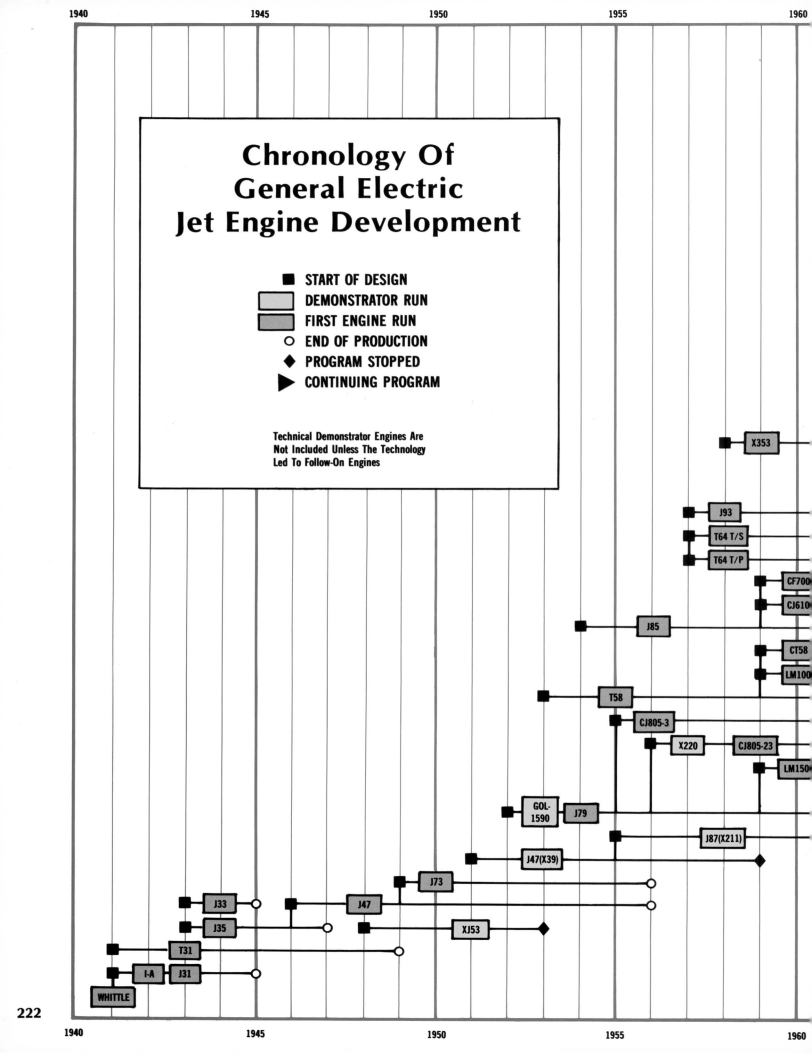

Chronology Of
General Electric
Jet Engine Development

■ START OF DESIGN
□ DEMONSTRATOR RUN
▨ FIRST ENGINE RUN
○ END OF PRODUCTION
◆ PROGRAM STOPPED
▶ CONTINUING PROGRAM

Technical Demonstrator Engines Are
Not Included Unless The Technology
Led To Follow-On Engines

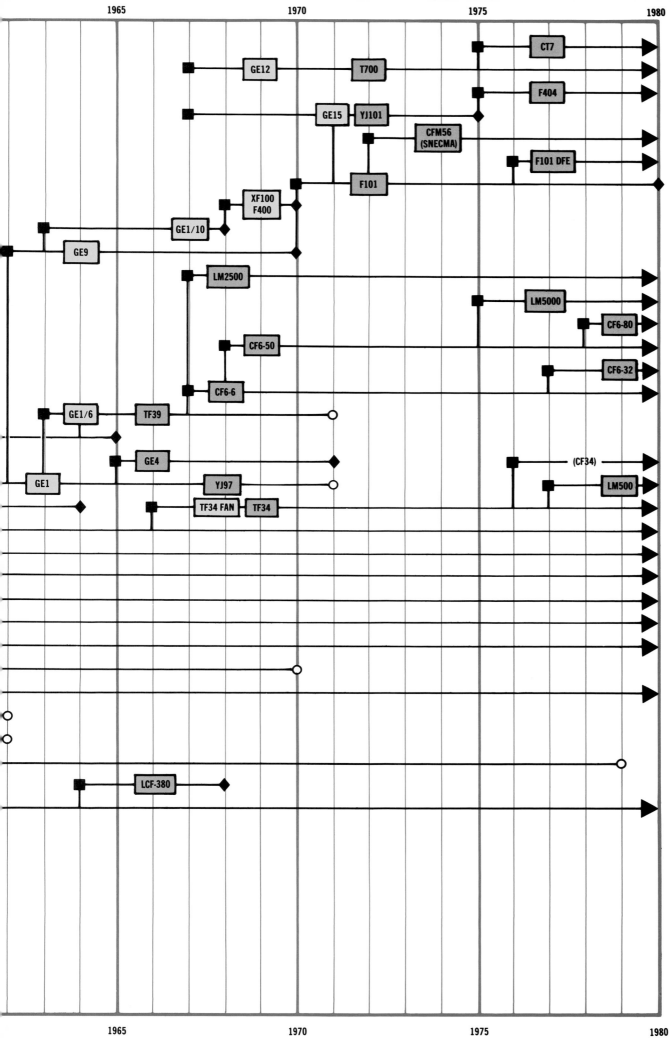

BIBLIOGRAPHY

American Aviation, "Design Trends in Jet Engine," 1953

American Heritage, "History of Flight," 1962

Aviation Age, "No Ceiling On Progress," 1953

Business Week, "Getting Along on a Lean Diet," 1954

Edmonds, I.G., "Jet and Rocket Engines," 1973

Elfun Society, General Electric, Algonquin Chapter, "The Edison Era, 1876-1892," "The Steinmetz Era, 1892-1923," "On the Shoulders of Giants, 1924-1946."

Encyclopaedia Britannica, Flight, 1768-1968

Encyclopaedia Britannica, Turbines History

Fortune, "GE's Hard-Driving Jockey in the Great Jet Engine Race," 1966

Fortune, "How a Great Corporation Got out of Control," 1962

General Electric Aircraft Engine Group News Bureau—releases

General Electric, "How We Grew," 1951

General Electric Jet Times, 25th Anniversary tabloid, 1967

Gilbert, James, "The Great Planes," 1970

Gilpatric, R.L., 10th Anniversary of U.S. Jet Flight, speech, 1952

Heiman, Grover, "Jet Pioneers," 1963

Kane, "Famous First Facts," 1976

LaPierre, C.W., "Power for Progress in the Air," speech, Newcomen Society, 1954

LaPierre, C.W., 10th Anniversary of U.S. Jet Flight, speech, 1952

Legacy of Leadership, A Pictorial History of Trans World Airlines, 1971

Loebelson, Robert, "To the Edge of Space," manuscript, 1962

Moss, Sanford A., "History of Gas Turbines for Aviation," paper, 1944

Neumann, Gerhard, interviews, 1965-79

O'Brien, M.P., interviews, 1975

Parker, Jack S., interviews, 1975

Rawlings, Lt. Gen. E.W., 10th Anniversary of U.S. Jet Flight, speech, 1952

Storer, J.D., "A Simple History of the Steam Turbine," 1969

Travers, W.R., interviews, 1975-1979

Travers, W.R., "The General Electric Aircraft Engine Story," manuscript, 1978

Tryckare, Tre. "The Lore of Flight," 1970

Whittle, Sir Frank, "Jet, the Story of a Pioneer," 1953

Wilson, C.E., 10th Anniversary of U.S. Jet Flight, speech, 1952

World Book Encyclopedia, various articles

Photo acknowledgment: All photographs and illustrations in *Seven Decades of Progress* were researched and compiled under the direction of R. Eric Falk, who served as photo editor. The editors gratefully acknowledge the following companies, agencies and individuals for their cooperation in helping to provide the extensive graphic material contained in the book: Airbus Industrie; Bath Iron Works; Bell Aerospace; Bell Aircraft; Bell Helicopters; Boeing; Canadair; Cessna; Chance Vought; Chase Aircraft; Consolidated Vultee; Convair; Dassault; deHavilland of Canada; Douglas; Elfun Society; Fairchild Republic; Fiat (Aeritalia); Gates Learjet; General Dynamics; Grumman; Hamburger Flugzeugbau; Hughes Helicopters; Israel Aircraft Industries; Italian Navy; Jet Pioneers Association; Kaman Aircraft; Kawasaki; Lockheed; Martin; McDonnell Douglas; North American Aviation; Northrop; Pan American World Airways; Republic Aviation; Rockwell; Ryan Aeronautical; SAAB; Shin Meiwa; Sikorsky; Harry Slone; SNECMA; John W. R. Taylor; Teledyne Ryan; Trans World Airlines; Hans von Ohain; Sir Frank Whittle. In addition, the editors are grateful to the following U.S. Government agencies: U.S. Air Force; U.S. Army; U.S. Coast Guard; U.S. Marine Corps; U.S. Navy; plus the Federal Aviation Administration and the National Aeronautics and Space Administration.

The credit for the majority of photos in this book must go to the dedicated group of General Electric photographic artists who have, over the years, captured on film the pictorial depiction of the seven decades of GE progress in aircraft turbine technology. Some of these GE professionals include Jack Hessler, Howard Hood, Sterling Keeton, Gene Mefford, Dick Miller, Jerry Reagan, Mike Reilly, Bill Thompson, Mel Tucker, Tom Ware, Ed Wesley, Leroy Whitehead, John Wiesman, Dick Willson, Lloyd Winter, plus John Eramo, George Garian, Allan Hunt, Robert Jacques, Thomas Kobuszewski, Leonard Thomas, and Henry Vienneau.

INDEX

INDEX

INDEX